Code
for
Classifiers

Principles governing
the consistent placing of books
in a system of
classification

WILLIAM STETSON MERRILL

Second Edition

AMERICAN LIBRARY ASSOCIATION
CHICAGO

Standard Book Number 8389-0027-5 (1939)

Copyright 1939 by the
American Library Association
Published October 1939

Ninth Printing, March 1969

DEDICATED
TO
MY WIFE

Contents

Foreword

The present work is an attempt to formulate some principles by which consistency may be maintained by the classifier in assigning books to their appropriate places in a system of classification. While this code is not entirely independent of existing systems of classifying human knowledge, it is not bound up with any such system and may be applied to any one of them. This adaptability arises from the fact that the code is concerned, not with questions as to the right sequence of subjects, but with the principles by which books are to be assigned consistently and suitably to places in a system of book classification.

The book, in its first edition of 1928, was a revision and rearrangement of the *Code for classifiers* issued in a mimeographed edition in 1914, which appeared under the auspices of a special committee of the American Library Association, appointed in 1912 to consider the preparation of such a code. Copies of this compilation of tentative rules were sent out to a number of libraries, library schools, and classifiers, with a request for comment and criticism; and the data received in response to this appeal were incorporated into the text with the permission of the librarians of the institutions to which the decisions were credited.

The author was indebted for these early contributions especially to the following: to Miss Julia Pettee, then head classifier of the Union Theological Seminary, who supplied some excellent definitions and whose rearrangement in classified form of the topics treated in the code was adopted; to the late Miss Dorkas Fellows, who indicated the divergencies from the rules of the code in the practice of the New York State Library; to Miss Ida F. Farrar, of the Public Library of Springfield, Mass., for criticisms; to Miss Grace O. Kelley, then classifier of the John Crerar Library, for rulings on scientific subjects; to Mr. P. L. Windsor, director of the University of Illinois Library, at whose invitation the subject of the code was first presented in the form of lectures delivered by the author, in March, 1912, before the library school of that university; to Mr. J. C. Bay, librarian of the John Crerar Library, and to Mr. George B. Utley, librarian of the Newberry Library, for counsel and unfailing encouragement. Opportunity to formulate the rules and prepare the work for publication was afforded the author while he was classifier at the Newberry Library.

The *Code for classifiers*, as now issued in a new edition, is much expanded. Sixty-five new sections, containing nearly 200 new rules, have been added; several definitions and rules have been rewritten; and classification procedure by the Library of Congress and by the editors of the Decimal classification has been recorded in cases of divergence by those systems from the procedure recommended in the rules.

The new rules introduced into this edition are based upon replies received to a circular letter suggested and distributed by Mr. Everett O. Fontaine, chief, Publishing Department of the American Library Association. This appeal, addressed to librarians, directors of library schools, teachers of classification, and classifiers in the larger libraries, asked the recipients to report upon any new problems of classification that had arisen at their libraries during recent years. Such new topics as Fascism, Nazism, political communism, economic emergency measures, so called, of the federal government, as well as new subjects in science, were suggested as calling for new rulings in the code.

The 30 replies to the 100 letters mailed out contained, aside from replies to the questions asked, an unexpectedly rich supply of new rulings upon both new and old problems. The Los Angeles and Queens Borough public libraries sent transcripts of many decisions made and recorded by their classifiers during the past 10 or 15 years. These decisions, adapted by the author to the phraseology of the code, have been incorporated into the text, either as rules or as alternative modes of classifying the material mentioned. Queries on scientific matters, sent by correspondents, were submitted to the John Crerar Library and the rulings thereon have largely been adopted. Rules derived from the reported practice of a given library have been credited to that library.

The first six sections of the code have been rewritten in the line of suggestions made by Miss Susan Grey Akers, director of the School of Library Science at the University of North Carolina. Rules for the treatment of publications of learned societies embody decisions made regarding certain types of material cited by Miss Esther Anell, serial reviser at the University of Illinois Library. Acting upon a plea by Miss Agnes Camilla Hansen, associate director and teacher in Pratt Institute School of Library Science, that the number of examples be made more plentiful for the benefit especially of students of classification, examples for all of the new rules have been cited. Printed cards for examples illustrating the rules have been secured through the kindness of Mr. Charles H. Hastings, former chief (now consultant) of the Card Division of the Library of Congress. Selection of the cards was entrusted by Mr. Hastings to his assistant, Mr. Laud R. Pitt, who with excellent judgment selected titles, often several to a rule, of works falling under the rules. Printed cards were also obtained for examples cited in the first edition so far as the works mentioned were in the Library of Congress. The author, now retired from active library work and living remote from the great libraries, would have been unable to introduce into the code the desirable features mentioned without the ever-ready and efficient aid of Mr. Hastings, who also sent him a full set of the schedules of classification of the Library of Congress.

The new rules were submitted to Mr. Clarence W. Perley, then chief (now retired) of the Classification Division of the Library of Congress, and to Mr. Myron W. Getchell, associate editor of the Decimal classification, who were asked to indicate the treatment given to the material by the two systems respectively. Mr. Getchell, who had been deputed by Miss Dorkas Fellows, shortly before her death, to answer the inquiries, also checked the references to the Dewey system in the first edition of the code. The author has compared all of the rulings of the code with the practice of the Library of Congress and of the Decimal classification, so far as this practice was revealed in schedules of classification, by comparison of class numbers for examples cited, and through correspondence. Classification by both systems of the examples given in the first edition has been indicated less completely in the absence of available data; and as the purpose of the rules has been to state directions simply and clearly, occasional variations in the handling of the examples have been ignored as tending to confuse the student.

The relationship in general of the rules of the code to the policy of the Decimal Classification Section, and to that of the Library of Congress, has been formulated by Mr. David Judson Haykin and Miss Julia C. Pressey in the following terms:

The absence of notes stating that the practice in either the L.C. or the D.C. system varies from a given rule indicates ordinarily that the system permits classification under the rule. But it does not necessarily mean that the system provides only the one given place for the subject, or that it recommends that given place to the exclusion of others, when established policy, or convenience, or some other factor makes classification elsewhere more practicable for an individual library.

Two features of the old edition have been eliminated from the new edition: (1) Dewey numbers printed opposite main headings to show the sequence of topics, and (2) references to the A.L.A. *Survey of libraries*. The omission of the latter was recommended by the Committee on Cataloging and Classification on the ground that the citations are either now out of date or are of slight didactic value. The printing of Dewey numbers has been the subject of divided opinion by critics and correspondents. The objections to their use, as stated by the editors of the Decimal classification, have been deemed decisive against their retention. An expanded table of contents in the new edition is intended to manifest sufficiently the arrangement of the book.

The manuscript has had the benefit of a close scrutiny by the members of the A.L.A. Committee on Cataloging and Classification, who returned it to the writer, accompanied by many suggestions and minor criticisms for which the writer wishes to express his indebtedness. No comment was made by the committee upon the rulings as such for the treatment of books, and the author assumes full responsibility for them as representing a fair consensus of professional opinion.

My acknowledgments are hereby expressed to all who have contributed to this second edition of the code. Much time and pains must have been given to the preparation of the data sent in by libraries and by individuals, and I deeply appreciate the generosity with which this aid has been rendered. I beg to mention personally, besides those already named, the following correspondents: Miss Harriet E. Penfield, classifier of the John Crerar Library; Miss Frances R. Foote, catalog department librarian at the Los Angeles Public Library; Miss Elizabeth S. Radtke, superintendent of cataloging at the Queens Borough Public Library; Miss Julia C. Pressey, assistant in charge of the Decimal Classification Section at the Library of Congress; Mr. James H. Conway, reference assistant at the Newberry Library. A copy of the latest edition of the Decimal classification, lent me by the Newberry Library, has proven indispensable. My wife has given me constant aid and counsel.

The *Code for classifiers* is now more than ever before, thanks to the generous cooperation of many professional workers in the field, a codification of widespread procedure in the classifying of books of certain types or treating of topics that present problems to the classifier. As a norm the code may safely be followed as representing, not the isolated opinions of the author, but the sound judgment of many competent classifiers.

W. S. M.

Oconomowoc, Wisconsin
April 1, 1939

List of Contributing Libraries

When mentioned in the text these libraries are referred to by the abbreviations or shortened names prefixed below

ABBREVIATION	NAME
Boston	Public Library of the City of Boston
California U.	Library, University of California
Cincinnati	Public Library of Cincinnati
Columbia U.	Columbia University Library
Franklin and Marshall C.	Franklin and Marshall College Library
Harvard U.	Harvard College Library
Illinois U.	University of Illinois Library
Indianapolis	Indianapolis Public Library
Iowa State C.	Iowa State College Library
John Crerar Library	John Crerar Library
L.C.	Library of Congress
Los Angeles	Los Angeles Public Library
Michigan U.	University of Michigan—Department of Library Science
New York State Library	New York State Library
Nebraska U.	University of Nebraska Library
Newberry Library	Newberry Library
North Carolina U.	University of North Carolina—School of Library Science
Pratt Institute	Pratt Institute—School of Library Science
Princeton U.	Princeton University Library
Queens Borough	Queens Borough Public Library
Syracuse U.	Syracuse University Library
Temple U.	Temple University—Sullivan Memorial Library
Wesleyan U.	Wesleyan University—Olin Library

* * * * * * * *

D.C.	Decimal clasification and relativ index. Edition 13. 1932.

Code for Classifiers

GENERAL PRINCIPLES OF CLASSIFYING BOOKS

1 Definition

Classification of books may be defined as the art of assigning books to their proper places in a system of classification in which the various subjects of human inquiry, or the descriptions of human life in its various aspects, are grouped according to their likeness or relation to one another.

2 Principle of classification

Class a book where it will be permanently useful, not where it may serve only a temporary need.

The classifier should not be led to disregard this principle to meet casual needs of the library or passing interests of the public, which may be met in other ways. Decisions should be made by principle; procedure should be consistent; and the point should steadily be kept in mind that the purpose of classification is not to place the book where it may be looked for, but where the *matter* in it may be looked for. The author catalog, and to some extent the subject catalog, are made for the purpose of finding the book; classification is concerned exclusively with its contents.

3 Characteristic chosen

Class a book ordinarily by subject.

Certain alternative characteristics may, when desirable, be chosen to determine the classification. Such characteristics are: date, binding, language, literary form, class of reader for whom the work is intended. Rules governing the selection of such alternative classifications will be found under their respective headings.

Never class a book by the title alone. When two subjects are mentioned in the title connected by "and," ascertain the relation of these subjects as brought out in the book and class accordingly. Cf. Relation: 15.

4 Intent of the author

Class a book primarily according to the intent of the author in writing it.

The subject of a book may be said to be the topic that the author sets out to treat and does treat after his fashion. The intent of the author thus determines *what the book is about.* This intent is indicated by the title-page, preface, table of contents, and the text of the book. A book is generally classed most usefully according to the intent of the author; for the topic that he intends to treat is its main subject. Other subjects may be introduced incidentally or to support the thesis of the book; but they do not constitute the value of the book as a whole.

D.C. says to class usually by the "predominant tendency" of a book.

5 Close classification

(a) Class a book by the most specific topic that will express the character of the book.

(b) Subordinate place to topic. If *no* local subdivisions are provided under a subject, class a work treating of local conditions directly under the topic, not under a larger division for which local subdivisions *are* provided.

The tendency which some classifiers, as well as some system-makers, have of making exceptions to the rule of "topic first, place second" is contrary to the principle of close classification. Country subdivisions are seldom subdivided by topic; hence when works on special topics are placed under the country subdivisions of larger scope than the topic, these works are lost. If every special topic is given a place, however, local subdivision under it is easily made, if desirable. Cf. Local treatment of topics: 42-44.

6 Modification for special needs

Modify a rule of classification of books when necessary or desirable to meet special needs or types of service.

Modification should be done with deliberation and consistency, and the classifier should bear in mind the effect of departure from the procedure advised upon other rules of the code. Modification of the rules given will naturally be made by libraries of special scope or serving special constituencies. The rules here presented are meant for the general library, but they may usefully be taken by any library as a basis of consistency, subject to change with times and conditions. Departure from the code is easy; subordination of all rules to expediency means chaos.

DIRECTIONS APPLICABLE TO ANY CLASS
OF MATERIAL

7 Argumentative facts

Facts or data of whatever kind, selected to prove a point or policy: Class strictly according to the intent of the author, disregarding the nature of the material used. E.g. *Power of the federal judiciary over legislation.* By J. Hampton Dougherty (New York, 1921). A historical argument against recall of judges, hence to be classed as a topic, *judicial recall,* under federal judiciary, not under legislation.

The data marshalled by an author to prove his point may be historical, political, literary, or what not; while the point to be proved is of quite different character.

8 Aspects of a subject

Class under the subject illustrated, not under the subject suggested by the aspect unless the latter really expresses the subject matter of the book. E.g. (1) *Social aspects of education.* By Irving King (New York, 1913). Class under education, not under sociology. But (2) *Religious aspect of philosophy.* By Josiah Royce (Boston, 1885). A work on the philosophy of religion.

9 Contrasted opinions or policies

A work contrasting two opinions, one advocated by the author and the other condemned by him: Class under the opinion or policy advocated by the author. E.g. *Naturalism or idealism.* By Rudolf Eucken (Cambridge, 1912). Class under idealism, which is advocated by the author.

10 Field of research

Results attained in a certain field of research: Class under the topic investigated without reference to the character of the data or means employed. E.g. *Abstract Bulletin* of the Physical Laboratory of the National Electric Light Association, Cleveland, Ohio. Class under electric lighting, although the researches are physical, in other words scientific rather than technological, but bearing upon electrical engineering.

11 Genetic (i.e. evolutionary) treatment of topics

Works treating of the origin of customs, institutions, or beliefs: Class under the topic so derived, or supposed to be so derived, not under its origins. E.g. (1) Myth as the origin of religion. Class under the history (or philosophy) of religion, not under mythology. (2) English common law as the source of American institutions. Class under American government.

12 History of a subject

Class under the specific heading even when that heading is not subdivided by subhead "history," in preference to classing in the subdivision "history" of a more general subject. E.g. *Nature in Italian art, a study of landscape backgrounds from Giotto to Tintoretto.* By Emma Gurney-Salter (London, 1912). Class under landscape painting, not under the history of Italian art, even though the technique of landscape painting may not be distinguished in the classification from its history.

The temptation to choose the subhead of the inclusive subject arises especially when the scope of the book is limited to a single country for which no subhead is made under the topic.

Example cited is classed by L.C. in landscape painting in Italy (ND1358).

Miss Pettee writes: "In general the history of a topic is considered a special method of treating the topic and should go with other material on the topic. For example, class a history of physiological botany with physiological botany and not with the general history of botany or the general history of biology. The Library of Congress classification does not always adhere to this rule but sometimes collects the history of various topics under inclusive headings; but I think the general practice of classifiers is against this."

The 13th edition of the Decimal classification provides for form headings, e.g. *history, periodicals,* under subdivisions as well as under the larger divisions. "Divisions introduced by 0, 00, or 000 may be annext to the number for *any* subject if 0 or 00 divisions are not already specifically provided under that subject."—p.1628.

13 Illustrative material

The term "illustrative" is used here in its primary signification, of serving to "explain by means of figures, examples, comparisons, and the like."—*(New standard dictionary)*.

(a) A work upon some specific topic, event, or institution "illustrative of" some larger or more general topic: Class under the specific topic. In other words, prefer the concrete to the abstract topic. E.g. *Origin and growth of religion as illustrated by the religion of the ancient Hebrews.* By C. G. Montefiore (London, 1892). Class under Jewish religion (or Old Testament), not with works on the origin of religion.

The Jewish religion is what the author is concretely treating. If the title had read: "The Jewish religion as an illustration of the growth of religion," the classifier would have no hesitation about classing the book under Jewish religion.

(b) A work illustrating a general or abstract topic by data relating to a single country or person: Class under the country or person. E.g. *The relations of Pennsylvania with the British government, 1696–1765.* By Winfred Trexler Root (University of Pennsylvania, 1912). Class under history of Pennsylvania, although the author states her purpose to be "to elucidate the nature of British imperialism . . . during the eighteenth century," by the treatment of Pennsylvania. The concrete prevails over the abstract subject here.

(c) A work in which material to illustrate a topic has been gathered from several sources: Class under the subject illustrated. E.g. *Symbol and satire in the French revolution.* By Ernest F. Henderson (New York, 1912). Class under French Revolution.

14 Method vs. Subject-matter

(a) A work treating of the results of applying a given method, hypothesis, or theory to the investigation of a given subject: Class under the subject investigated, not under the method of investigation. E.g. *The ethical import of Darwinism.* By Jacob Gould Schurman (New York, 1887). Class under ethics, not under Darwinism, because it applies evolution to explain ethics.

Example cited is classed by L.C. in *evolutionary ethics* (BJ1311) under philosophy ; so also by D.C. (171.7).

(b) Development of physical methods for exploring biological materials: Class by the material, not by the method. E.g. Biological determination of vitamins. Class in physiological chemistry.—(Iowa State College Library).

(c) Magneto-optic and spectroscopic methods: Class with the matter of research.

Iowa State College Library writes: "On the advice of our physics department, we have so far kept the few publications on this topic with physics, but the solution is not entirely satisfactory." As spectroscopic methods are used to determine various matters of research, the rule as given is in line with the principle of classing by effect, not by cause ; end attained, not means of attaining it ; result, not method of reaching it. If, however, one method is described for reaching several results, the rule will be reversed, as classification can bring out only one topic at a time.

Cf. Applications of one science to another : 173.

15 Relation

When a book treats of more than one subject, or of the relation existing between two or among several subjects : Determine what this relation is and class according to the following rules.

Even when a symbol or number is used to express the relation of two subjects, e.g. the colon (:) in the Brussels classification, or the form number (0001) in the D.C., the classifier must decide to which of two class numbers this symbol is to be affixed.

(a) If the work treats of two factors, one of which is represented as acting upon or influencing the other : Class under the subject *influenced or acted upon.* E.g. (1) The influence of the Icelandic sagas upon English literature. Class under English literature. (2) Influence of the climate of California upon its literature. Class under literature.

This is a very important rule and one that has been strangely overlooked or disregarded by writers on classification. An experience of many years in applying it convinces the author of its entire practicability and usefulness.

(b) If one factor is represented as the source, cause or formative agency of the other: Class under the factor so derived or resulting. E.g. (1) Myth as a source of religion. Class under the origin of religion. (2) Economic conditions as a cause of war. Class under war, but class economic *effects* of war under economics.

Relation is often expressed on title-pages by connecting two topics by the conjunction "and" without further specifying the relationship. E.g. Art and ritual, which may mean the way in which art has grown out of ritual; Norse literature and English literature, which may mean the Norse sources of English literature; Shaftesbury and Wieland, indebtedness of Wieland to Shaftesbury; Cardinal Aleman and the Great Schism, share that Cardinal Aleman had in the movement. The classifier should first determine the meaning of "and" before attempting to classify and should never accept the first word given on the title-page as determining the subject of the book.

(c) If the subjects are practically subdivisions of some larger inclusive subject: Class under the inclusive subject.

(d) If the two subjects are merely coordinated, e.g. electricity and magnetism treated in the same volume: Class always under the first subject, unless the second decidedly preponderates.

(e) Literary influence of authors. See that heading under Literature: 281, 292.

16 Special reference to a subject

Works treating of some topic "with special reference to" a country, person, or subject: Class under the more restricted topic. E.g. *Elizabethan demonology . . . with special reference to Shakespeare and his works.* By Thomas Alfred Spalding (London, 1880). Class under Shakespeare.

Example cited is classed by L.C. in demonology (BF1517.G7).

SPECIAL FORMS OR TYPES OF LITERARY MATERIAL

17 Commemorative volumes. Festschriften

Collected essays presented to an author, teacher, or other distinguished person and published in his honor: Class under the main subject covered by the volume, which is usually the field of knowledge in which the person honored is eminent.

18 Dialogs

Works discussing serious topics of historical, philosophical, or scientific nature under the form of dialog: Class under the topic unless the intent of the author is plainly literary and not informational. E.g. *Evenings with the skeptics*. By John Owen (London, 1881. 2v.). Written in the form of dialogs with fictitious setting, but interspersed with philosophic essays and of informational value.

Example cited is classed by L.C. in *scepticism* (B837) under philosophy.

19 Dissertations

Treat like pamphlets. See Pamphlets: 24. For doctoral dissertations see 167.

20 Facsimiles

(a) Facsimiles of printed books (except incunabula): Class with the originals or where the originals would be classed. E.g. photostats of old newspapers, or of rare books.

(b) Facsimiles of incunabula: Class with incunabula, not under the subject of the book. The work is nearly always of typographic interest only.

(c) Facsimiles of manuscripts. See Manuscripts: 59.

21 Festival and holiday addresses

Class with other works on the festivals or under the subject which these anniversaries commemorate. Cf. Fourth of July addresses: 363, and Thanksgiving Day addresses: 29.

The alternative is to class with orations, which does not bring out the subject matter; while to separate those having importance for the subject from those useful only as specimens of oratory is impracticable.

22 **Inaugural addresses of college presidents, professors, and public officials**

Class with other works on the institution, not attempting to determine the precise topic or theme of the discourse. E.g. *Rectorial addresses delivered before the University of Edinburgh, 1859–1899* (London, 1900).

This rule will apply usually to individual addresses as well as to collections. The alternative of placing them strictly by the theme of the address is not so good for the reasons: (1) The subject is often vaguely defined; (2) the topic is usually treated largely in its bearing upon the institution or its methods or functions; (3) the addresses are integrally a part of the history of the institution.

Example cited is classed by L.C. in *addresses* (LF1047.5) under University of Edinburgh.

23 **Newspapers, Bound**

Newspapers differ so radically from ordinary periodicals or books that there are good reasons for treating them as a distinct type of material. They are unlike books and yet are used for research, like inscriptions on stone or plaster, original coins, or other material not easily coordinated with books. They are issued daily; or, if weekly, they are much larger in size than weekly periodicals. Hence the issues of a year may require twelve or even more bindings, necessitating special shelves, rooms, tables, and mechanical appliances for making the volumes available to the public. The two points that specially concern the classifier are: What is the distinction between a weekly newspaper and a weekly periodical? What arrangement to make of newspapers?

(a) Class a weekly serial of newspaper size with newspapers; one of smaller size with periodicals unless plainly only a purveyor of news.

Mechanical as this rule appears, the experience of classifiers will, it is believed, approve it.

(b) Class a weekly periodical issued by a newspaper, under a separate title and of different format, as a periodical. E.g. *Liberty,* formerly issued by the *Chicago Tribune.*

(c) Class a weekly supplement, issued as an integral part of the Sunday or other issue of the newspaper, even when it has a separate title, as the supplement to that newspaper. E.g. *American Weekly,* which is a syndicated supplement

distributed by 21 newspapers. Class with the newspaper issuing it.

(d) Arrange newspapers first by country in which issued, disregarding the language; secondly by city, either in
one alphabet or alphabetically under states or provinces;
thirdly alphabetically by the significant word in the title.
E.g. *Chicago Daily News* would be classed United States—
Illinois (or Chicago directly)—Chicago—News, the words
"Chicago" and "daily" being disregarded in the alphabetical
arrangement by title. *Illinois Staats-Zeitung* would come
under U.S.—Illinois, not with German newspapers published in Germany.

24 Pamphlets

(a) Original editions of rare or otherwise valuable
pamphlets—tracts, controversial treatises, addresses, or
other pieces—published separately: Class and bind separately like books by subject.

(b) Reprints of rare pamphlets numbered in series:
Class by the subject covered by the series. E.g. A reprint of
economic tracts (Baltimore, 1903–1915).

(c) Serial pamphlets: Class together by the subject
covered. E.g. *Farmers' bulletins,* issued by the U.S. Department of Agriculture.

(d) Independent pamphlets: Class like books.

If of considerable and permanent value, bind and shelve like books;
otherwise file by subject in vertical files or place on shelf by subject,
protected by cardboard covers tied with tape. Pamphlet boxes are
less desirable because the pamphlets become bent from sagging or
torn from frequent insertions.

25 Series

(a) Series formed to cover a certain field and bring together works that, if independent, would be classed outside
of the field of the series: Class together. E.g. (1) The
Humanists' library, edited by Lewis Einstein (Boston,
1907–1914). This is an example of a series that brings together, with a selective purpose, works of different content

but characterized by being the writings of humanists, and as such of importance and special interest to students of humanism. (2) The Shakespeare classics (London, 1912). Class together because the intent of the series is to bring together from various sources works illustrating the works of Shakespeare as originals or analogs; these works if classed strictly by subject, e.g. Lodge's *Rosalynde*, would be scattered so far apart as to defeat the purpose of the series.

(b) Series arranged in chronological order or according to some systematic scheme: Class together. E.g. The Chronicles of America series (New Haven, 1919–1921).

Such series have far more significance for the whole ground covered by them than would a series of books arranged alphabetically by authors, whether numbered by volume or not. Series of the kind mentioned are thus in a way comprehensive works in several volumes, each covering one period or aspect of the subject.

(c) Biographical series covering one field of knowledge or one school of thought: Class together. E.g. (1) English philosophers; (2) Fromanns Klassiker der philosophie (Stuttgart, 1910–   ). The latter series includes such diverse subjects as Aristotle, Carlyle, Mill and Goethe, each of whom is treated primarily as a philosophic thinker.

(d) Geographical series intended to include all the colonies of a nation: Class together. E.g. The English people overseas (Boston, 1912. 5v.). As one volume treats of the American Colonies, another of British India, another of Britain in the tropics, the set should be classed together as history of British possessions past and present; its specific subject is thus a history of British *colonies* as such.

New York State Library scatters such series by individual country.

(e) Series of texts in the less-known languages, or confined to a certain period in the history of a language: Class together. E.g. (1) University of Wales: Welsh texts (London, 1912–   ); (2) Early English Text Society (London, 1, 1864–   ). To scatter the works composing the latter series would be tragic for the student of early English literature.

(f) Series bringing together works exhibiting the teach-

ings or tenets of a certain religious body, political party, or
school of thought: Class together. E.g. *Publications* of the
Wyclif Society.

(g) Series within series, i.e. one that has its own numbering and also the numbering of the larger series of which it
is a part: Leave within the inclusive series. E.g. (1) *Mis-
cellanea,* forming scattered volumes of the *Publications* of
the Catholic Record Society (London), but bearing its
own volume numbering. (2) *Berichte* der Commission für
erforschung des östlichen Mittelmeers, which form scattered volumes of the *Denkschriften* of the Vienna Academy.

If the included series were classed separately the larger series
would become a broken set. But if the inclusive series has no serial
numbering, prefer the included series, especially if significant of some
special topic or field. E.g. the Shakespeare classics, which form one
section of the Shakespeare library. Class in sources and analogs of
Shakespeare's plays, not with general collections on Shakespeare.

(h) Series in which some or all of the numbered volumes
contain more than one work in each: Class together. Cf.
Serial monographs of a similar character: 27e.

(i) Series composed of tracts, pamphlets, or small volumes which it is desirable to bind collectively: Class together. E.g. (1) A reprint of economic tracts (Baltimore,
1903–15); (2) Catholic Truth Society, *Publications.*

(j) Series composed of numbered leaflets: Class together. E.g. Publications of the U.S. Department of Agriculture.

(k) Series of merely current or temporary usefulness as
series: Scatter by subject. E.g. Home university library of
modern knowledge.

The passing value of having such series together may be met by
shelving them together.

(1) Other series: Scatter by subject.
Cf. Debaters: 36.

26 Serials of varying character or contents

Keep together, either leaving the whole set under the
original classification, even though unsuited to the later

volumes of the series; or changing the whole set to a new location. E.g. *Current History,* originally published by the *New York Times.* This periodical began as *Current History of the European War* and after the close of the war became a general magazine of current events.

Example cited is classed by L.C. as a periodical (D501) under European war.

27 **Academy and learned society publications**

Two questions arise in regard to this type of publication: (1) Shall the form number (e.g. 06 in the D.C.) be used for monographic publications which are like individual books except that they are issued with serial numbers? (2) Shall the sections or "classes" (klassen) of academies be kept by field or subject covered or shall they be kept together?

(a) Annals, bulletins, proceedings, transactions and other publications serially numbered: Keep together under the subject that expresses the scope of the academy or society as a whole, using the form number. E.g. (1) British Academy, London, *Proceedings.* (2) Huguenot Society of London, *Proceedings;* also its *Publications.* (3) Académie des inscriptions et belles-lettres, Paris, *Comptes rendus.* (4) Académie des sciences, Paris, *Comptes rendus.*

Examples cited are classed: (1) by L.C. in academies (AS122.L5); so also by D.C. (062). (2) by L.C. in Huguenots (BX9450) under religion; so also by D.C. (284.5). (3) by L.C. in academies (AS162.P315); so also by D.C. (064). (4) by L.C. in science (Q46); so also by D.C. (506.244).

(b) Publications issued without serial or volume numbering: Scatter by subject.

(c) Publications issued serially by sections or classes (klassen): Class together under the subject expressing the scope of the academy or society as a whole. E.g. (1) Akademie der Wissenschaften, Vienna—Philosophisch-historische Classe, *Denkschriften.* (2) Akademie der Wissenschaften—Mathematisch-naturwissenschaftliche Classe, *Denkschriften.* (3) Académie des sciences, des lettres et des beaux-arts de Belgique, which has three classes: beaux-arts, lettres . . . . , sciences.

This rule keeps together publications of the same society which would not only be widely separated by the subjects which they cover but would be separated by a purely arbitrary mode of publication. The same academy may begin by issuing all of its publications in a single series; then two classes may combine publications in one series or in two, three or more. Even if the serial publications of the scientific class of an academy are placed on the science shelves, they are not consulted without the guidance of analytical cards or printed references to exact volume and page contained in bibliographical indexes. Practically all such learned papers or articles are so indexed and may more easily be located when kept together.

(d) Monographic serials, i.e. serials designed to be issued indefinitely, the volumes of which, numbered consecutively. either form or comprise monographs. When monographic serials are issued by an academy or learned society: Class together with the other publications of the academy or society, using the form number for serials. E.g. (1) Florida State Historical Society, *Publications;* (2) Early English Text Society, *Publications.*

The alternative is to class serially issued monographs independently on the ground that they are books rather than papers or articles. This treatment fails to take account of the fact that such monographs are intended to appear in an indefinitely continued series. Such monographs, moreover, differ from papers and articles only in having greater length and wider scope; appearing in serial form they are likely to be indexed as serials and to be located by volume and number.

(e) Monographs or papers printed two or more combined in a volume of a series: Class by 27d.

The University of Illinois Library adduces examples of this type: "series in which each volume contains from six to a dozen or more articles; and there is nothing in the publications to indicate that these papers have been read as communications to the society." E.g. (1) *Annales Societatis zoolog.-botanicae fennicae Venamo.* (2) *Bulletin de la Société de biologie de Lettonie.* The fact that these papers may not have been read before the societies need not affect their classification; serial monographs are usually read only by title before sessions of learned societies.

Cf. series of similar character mentioned in 25h.

28 Special collections

Special collections, such as private libraries which have become parts of a public or institutional library; or collections made to cover all or certain features of a country or topic, which it is desirable to segregate in some way from the general collections: Class by subject but designate the book by some appropriate symbol prefixed to the call-number. Manuscripts may be treated in the same way. See Manuscripts: 58.

By this device either the books will automatically be brought together in one place and will stand arranged in classified order; or if scattered through the library, the symbol will designate them as belonging to the special collection.

29 Thanksgiving Day addresses

Class together rather than attempt to determine the precise topic of the address.

The desire on the part of Thanksgiving Day speakers to avoid triteness may lead them into a great variety of fields; but the topic is nevertheless supposed to have significance for the occasion. Cf. Festival and holiday addresses: 21.

30 Translations

(a) Poetry, history and works in any field except fiction: Class with the originals.

(b) Fiction: Class with originals.

In popular libraries class translations of fiction into English with English fiction.

FORM DIVISIONS

31 Cyclopedias and dictionaries

Class first by subject, secondly by form.

While this rule is almost a truism in library classification, yet it is subject to modification in the case of cyclopedias and dictionaries of somewhat wider scope or field of usefulness. The collection of books of general reference in the reading room may not improperly include cyclopedias of painting and handbooks of statistics arranged in one alphabet of authors; yet it is doubtful whether this arrangement is as useful as the classified arrangement.

"The various classifications provide for encyclopedic material of special topics under the topic, and as a rule this arrangement is decidedly preferable to any other. If, however, some special reason

makes it seem advantageous to bring encyclopedias of all kinds to-
gether, this may be done by assigning the class mark or stamp, as
'Ref.' (reference) before the number."—(Pettee).
Cf. Encyclopedic works treating of countries: 310d.

32 Indexes and calendars

Class with the topic indexed or calendared, not with the
bibliography of the topic. E.g. (1) Calendars of state
papers, issued by the Master of the Rolls. (2) Indexes of
parish registers.

The New York State Library classes calendars with bibliography.
D.C. does likewise when the index refers to several publications *not*
shelved together.

Example (1) is classed by L.C. in *sources* (DA25) under history
of England.

33 Periodicals

In the case of a periodical the difficulties are: (1) to determine the scope of the periodical, (2) to decide whether
to class it strictly by the subject or to place it with other
periodicals of somewhat wider scope. The University of
Illinois Library raises the question: "When should a
periodical be classified with the subject rather than in a periodical number?" In reply it may be said that as a periodical should be classed according to its scope, the class
number that best fits that scope should be used. Formerly
the form number for periodicals was used in the Decimal
classification only with the larger divisions; now that it
may be used "for any subject if 0 to 00 divisions are not
already specifically provided under that subject" (13th ed.,
p.1628), the notation may easily be made to express the
periodical issue of the work under any topic. The Library
of Congress provides specifically for periodicals under subjects, presumably wherever there is literature to be classed.

(a) Class a periodical according to its scope or by the
field that it covers. E.g. (1) *Harvard business review*. (2)
Electronics. (3) *U.S.S.R. in Reconstruction*. (4) *Invest-
ment banking*. (5) *Bird-lore*. Cf. History of a subject: 12,
note.

The scope of a periodical should be determined by (1) title; (2) editorial announcements; (3) contents. As periodicals are more likely to broaden their scope than to restrict it, it is better in cases of doubt to class by the broader of two fields. When the scope changes essentially, the subject catalog and suitable references serve to make the periodical known under its new scope. E.g. *Current History*, which started as *Current History of the European War*. There are decidedly practical difficulties in changing the call-number of a periodical every time it changes its scope or character.

Some libraries may prefer to class together all periodicals indexed in "Poole" in one alphabet for convenience. As the Wilson printed indexes to serials, however, include publications in many fields of knowledge, the same purpose is served by shelving the indexed serials in close proximity to the delivery desk.

(b) When a periodical changes title, keep it under the same call-number if the volume numbering is continued; but treat it as a new periodical, giving it a new number and if necessary a new classification, if the volume numbering begins anew. E.g. *Mid-America,* which continues with widened scope but continuous volume numbering, *Illinois Catholic Historical Review.*

This ruling may sound mechanical and arbitrary, but long experience with classing periodicals will confirm alike its simplicity and its practicability.

(c) Periodicals (general in scope) published in a language foreign to that of the country in which they appear: Class by language, placing them in a group by themselves, if desired, under the country. E.g. (1) The *East of Asia magazine,* a non-political illustrated quarterly (Shanghai, 1902–1906). Published by English residents in Shanghai, China. Class with English, not Chinese, periodicals. (2) *Deutscher volksfreund* (New York, 1871–1906). Class with German, not American, periodicals. Cf. Newspapers: 23.

(d) Monographs issued by periodicals: Class with the periodical when numbered serially; otherwise scatter by subject. E.g. *Zentralblatt für bibliothekswesen,* Beihefte. Class with the periodical.

The same reasons apply here as for serial monographs issued by societies: 27d–e.

BOOKS WRITTEN FOR ONE CLASS OF USER

34 Blind

Class books for the blind in a scheme of their own, or prefix to the classification number a symbol that will bring them together as a special collection.

Although these books will be read by none but the blind, their arrangement should be determined in a way to suit the convenience of the library staff handling them. Unless the collection is very extensive a broad adaptation of the classification used in the rest of the library is advisable.—(A.L.A. Committee).

L.C. keeps together books for the blind in a collection arranged by the form of type, e.g. Braille, New York point, Moon; under each form the books are placed in a broad classification following the system used in the library.

35 Children

Class by subject, but designate by some appropriate symbol, e.g., "J" for "juveniles" or "ch" for "children." Use ordinarily a broad classification.

L.C. keeps juvenile literature in a special collection.

36 Debaters

Series (and perhaps books) written especially for debaters will be usefully classed together, not scattered throughout the classification under the subject.

L.C. classes outlines with arguments by subject.

This is purely a practical device to bring conveniently together books that are used for a similar purpose, especially by school children.

37 Draftsmen and designers in special fields

Class under the subject illustrated by the book (architecture, engineering, designing of heraldic crests). E.g. (1) Engineering drawing, which is an integral part of the technique of engineering and should be classed there, not under drawing (unless the system brings all kinds of drafting together under drawing). (2) *Heraldry for craftsmen and designers*. By W. H. St. John Hope (London, 1913). Written to explain to makers of crests and coats of arms the meaning of heraldic language and symbols and thus a work on heraldry.

L.C. classes (1) in mechanical drawing (T351-) under technology. D.C. classes engineering drawings (620.04) under engineering. Example (2) is classed by L.C. in *heraldry in art* (CR31) under heraldry.

38 Technicians

Class with works on the technique of the profession for which the book is intended. E.g. (1) Mathematics for electricians. Class under electric engineering. (2) Accounting for special lines of business. Class under the business.

A book on mathematics for electricians includes only such portions of the science of mathematics as bear upon electric computations. It is thus a treatise on one branch of the technique of that profession, not a work on mathematics. Yet opinion is not unanimous upon this question. Cf. Mathematics for technicians: 177d, Theoretical-applied science: 197, and Business methods: 221.

Queens Borough writes: "This library follows Library of Congress class HF5686, classing in accounting when HF numbers are given, and with the topic when L.C. so designates. The reason that appears to justify this is that accounting should be classified with the topic only when the method described is definitely not applicable to any other subject." This practice would appear, however, to place a book where it *may* be used rather than where the author intends it to be used.

TIME DIVISIONS

39 Works upon any subject covering a limited period of time

Class first by subject, subdividing the subject by time divisions. If the topic is not important enough to subdivide, class such a work with other books on the subject rather than under the period division of a larger inclusive heading. Cf. Time divisions vs. Local divisions (under History): 309.

"Do not leave in general time divisions any material which may be classed by topic or which will go in local divisions. E.g. A work on Italian Renaissance art goes with Italian art, not under the general number for Renaissance art. Period divisions may be used, if desired, under topic or local division. The place or topic takes precedence over period division, with few exceptions. The Reformation period of church history is one of these exceptions."—(Pettee). The Renaissance is rather a period than a topic under countries. The case of the Reformation may be considered by some classifiers, however, as a *topic*, i.e. revolt against the Catholic Church, subdivided by the countries in which this movement occurred. L.C. subdivides Reformation by country (BR358–) except local; D.C. classes Reformation as period under country (274–).

40 Works covering more than one period subdivision of the classification

(a) If several periods are covered: Class either under the general heading or, if the period is less than a century, class by centuries. Cf. Reigns and centuries: 305.

Treat the century as beginning with the odd year and ending with the even hundred.

(b) If the work covers two periods for which provision is made in the classification: Class under the first, unless the second decidedly predominates.

Sometimes an author who aims to trace the causes or origins of events in one period will review the events of a preceding period with that intent. In that case class under the second period. New York State Library classes under the predominant period; if this period is doubtful, under the first.

41 Chronological sequence for books in certain classes

Arrange by date within the classification:

(a) Incunabula
(b) Bible texts
(c) Liturgical books
(d) Editions of the same work
(e) Scientific books in a scientific library

Convenient notations for books to be kept in order of date are: Biscoe numbers; Merrill numbers for dates; or the dates written out in full.

LOCAL TREATMENT OF TOPICS

42 Works treating a subject limited in scope to a single country or locality

(a) Class first by topic, secondly by local subdivision. E.g. (1) *Animal life in Italian painting*. By William Norton Howe (London, 1912). Class under painting of animals, not under Italian painting. (2) Internal revenue taxation in the United States. Class under internal revenue, whether subdivided by country or not, and not under taxation in the United States. Cf. Close classification: 5.

Examples cited are classed: (1) by L.C. under Italian painting (ND615), but provision is made for technique and history of special subjects, e.g. *animals* (ND1380) under painting. (2) L.C. classes internal revenue in *indirect taxes* (HJ5001–   ) subdivided by country.

(b) Works treating of local conditions exclusively: Class locally, whether the title reads so or not. E.g. *A history of university reform from 1800 A.D.* By A. I. Tillyard (Cambridge, 1913). Treats only of higher education in England, although the title suggests a wider field.

(c) Works manifestly designed to treat a topic in a general way, but using local data or illustrating the theme by describing local conditions: Class under the general topic.

In other words if local conditions form the theme of the book, class locally; if local conditions are merely illustrative of general principles, class with the general topic. If all books making use of local conditions to illustrate a general theme were to be treated as local in scope, there would be little literature left under the general topic. Such a question as "protection or free trade," if treated by an American, will deal largely with American conditions, if by an Englishman, it will be based on English conditions; yet the book may be a general treatment of the question.

43 History of the theory of a subject, treated locally

Class with theory, not history, of the subject, subdivided by country, if desired.

History of economic thought in England may be viewed in three ways: (1) as theory, (2) as history, (3) as English economics. If classed as theory, it would come (in Dewey) in 330.1; if classed as history of economic thought, it would come in 330.9; if classed as English economics, it would come in 330.942. By classing such a work in theory of economics, subdivided, if desired, by country, it is separated from literature of quite different scope, namely, economic conditions. Similarly, history of esthetics in England should be separated from history of art in England.

The John Crerar Library rule is: "Class the history of the political theory of a special country, e.g. history of Hindu political theories, under the history of political science in that country instead of under theory of political science in general. This would apply also under other subjects, e.g. history of Hindu statistical theories, history of Hindu economic theories, history of Hindu banking theories, etc. This decision is debatable. Some libraries have found it advisable to class such material either under the theory of the subject or under the history of the subject." Classing under theory always conforms to the principle: class by subject, subdividing by country. Theory, not economic conditions, is the subject here. Another example is: *International arbitration amongst the Greeks.* By Marcus Niebuhr Tod (Oxford, 1913). Class under international arbitration, not under Greek history or foreign relations.

44 Great Britain vs. England

If a distinction is made between Great Britain and England in classing books treating of one or the other: Class (a) books of travel strictly according to the territory covered; but (b) books in other fields under either England or Great Britain, as preferred, but without separation.

Separation in other subjects than travel is both impracticable and inconvenient. The term "British" is often used without definite connotation; even works that can be differentiated cover much the same field and are better classed in the same section. E.g. *A dictionary of English and folk-names of British birds.* By H. Kirke Swann (London, 1913). The bibliography given in this volume mentions his work upon "English" and twenty other works on "British" birds; yet most of the birds are English. History of Great Britain is largely England for the earlier period; international relations are handled in London and the three "kingdoms" act as one unit, so far as the classifier is concerned.

CLASSIFICATION UNDER SPECIAL SUBJECTS

BIBLIOGRAPHY

45 Definition and scope of the class

"Bibliography in its broadest sense treats of all that appertains to the outward form of books,—their materials, printing, publishing and care. Called by various names, this material is grouped together in all classifications. The term bibliography, however, is generally restricted to lists of books of various kinds, either covering many topics, —publishers' catalogs, dealers' lists, library catalogs; or restricted in scope."—(Pettee). Bibliographies covering but one field or topic of knowledge are in some systems grouped together by some scheme or arrangement; in others provision is made under each subject for its bibliography.

"Material in this class is concerned strictly with the history of books as books,—their editions, dates, and form; it is not concerned with discussion upon the ideas of the author. It is difficult sometimes to draw the line between the history of a book and the history of the subject matter of the book. But theoretically the latter has no place in bibliography; it belongs in history of literature, art, science or technology."—(Pettee).

46 Bibliography vs. Catalogs

Disregard the distinction between the bibliography of a subject and catalogs of books in some collection or collections relating to the subject. Class under bibliography of the topic. E.g. (1) *Books on the great war.* By F. W. T. Lange & W. T. Berry (London, 1915–). (2) *European war collection* [in] Princeton university library (Princeton, 1918). Class both under bibliography of the war.

The only objection to this ruling is that a collection of books belonging to an indivdual has a certain association with him, and one connected with an institution forms part of the resources of that institution; but the subject catalog, or even the author catalog, will bring out this aspect of the book.

L.C. has subhead, *catalogues,* under subjects in bibliography.

47 Literary history of a topic

Class with history, not bibliography, of the topic. E.g. (1) *English historical literature in the fifteenth century.* By Charles Lethbridge Kingsford (Oxford, 1913). Class in history of England, subdivision historiography. (2) *Essai sur l'histoire de l'idée de progrès jusqu'à la fin du xviii. siècle.* Par Jules Delvaille (Paris, 1910). A history of the idea, not of the literature, of progress; hence to be classed with history of the topic.

The alternative is classing such works in bibliography of the subject, which may be preferred if the work is largely a list of books.

Examples cited are classed: (1) by L.C. in sources of English history of the Lancaster-York period (DA240); (2) by L.C. in history of civilization (CB73).

48 Bibliography of individuals

(a) Bibliography of persons who are not writers or not ranking as such: Class in bibliography of individuals. E.g. *Bibliography of Napoleon.* By F. Kircheisen (London, 1902).

(b) Bibliography of individual writers: Class in literature when their collected works and works about them are classed there. E.g. *Chaucer, a bibliographical manual.* By Eleanor P. Hammond (New York, 1908).

Example cited is classed by L.C. in *personal bibliography* (Z8164).

(c) Bibliography of writers whose writings are classed by subject: Class in subject bibliography. E.g. *Bibliography of the works of Father Louis Hennepin.* By Victor H. Paltsits (Chicago, 1903.) Class in bibliography of travel in the Mississippi Valley.

The alternative of classing all bibliography of individual writers together instead of by the subject of their writings may be preferred on the ground that the personal interest outweighs the subject.

L.C. classes in personal bibliography (Z8000–) bibliography of individuals (except musical composers); D.C. classes bibliography of individuals together in one alphabet of persons (012) "unless clearly limited in some subject, e.g. artists or musicians, when it is classed in bibliography of the subject."—(D.C. editors).

New York State Library rule is, with very few exceptions, to class bibliography of writers in that special section (D.C. 012), not with the collected works of the author or under the subject illustrated by them. This is undoubtedly the easiest place to find the bibliography of an author. The decision will rest largely upon whether subject bibliography is kept together or is scattered by subject.

If a distinction is made between history of an author's writings and bibliography of his works, the books can be divided only by literary form; lists of titles in alphabetical or chronological sequence being treated as bibliography, and narrative text being treated as biography.

49 Local bibliography (Bibliography of books about a place)

Class with bibliographies of works published *in* that place, unless limited to one aspect of the place, e.g. travel, art, literature. In other words, mix subject bibliography with national bibliography when the scope is general in content

but local in extent. E.g. (1) *Bibliography of Rhode Island
. . . publications relating to Rhode Island.* By J. R. Bart-
lett (Providence, 1864). (2) *Rhode Island imprints . . .
1727–1800* (Providence, 1915).

A possible reason for separation of the two classes of books,
namely, that works about a place may include foreign publications,
is outweighed by the consideration that works published in a place include a still larger proportion of works concerning it in one way or
another.

New York State Library classes bibliographies of miscellaneous
works about a place with bibliographies of the *history* of the place.
Cutter, on the other hand, would class general bibliography of books
about a place with bibliography of *description* of the place.

The author's experience, covering many years, in mixing bibliography of works printed *in* a place with bibliography of books *about*
it, satisfies him as to the wisdom of the above rule.

Examples cited are classed: (1) and (2) by L.C. in bibliography
of Rhode Island (Z1331) under national bibliography.

50 National bibliography vs. Subject bibliography

A work of bibliography covering works printed in a country as well as works treating of it but printed elsewhere:
Class under national bibliography.

L.C. classes both general bibliography of a country and special
bibliography of its literature, biography, history and description under
national bibliography; but bibliography of its art, music, agriculture,
geology, etc., in subject bibliography.

New York State Library classes such works under subject bibliography "unless the national feature clearly predominates." D.C.
does likewise.

51 Printing vs. Bibliography

(a) Local lists of printers or printing presses, with or
without titles of books printed, when arranged by printers
and containing biographical data: Class under printing.
E.g. *The early Massachusetts press, 1638–1711.* By George
Emory Littlefield (Boston, 1907. 2v.). Class under printing in Massachusetts.

(b) Lists of publications of a country or state, arranged
by authors or subjects: Class in national bibliography. E.g.
A century of printing; the issues of the press in Pennsyl-

vania, 1685–1784. By Charles R. Hildeburn (Philadelphia, 1885–86. 2v.). Class under local bibliography.

A distinction must be made unless the classifier is satisfied to leave vacant the sections of printing in a special country or place, classing all lists of books printed in a country or place under national or local bibliography.

52 Subject bibliography

Class subject bibliography in the division of bibliography or with the subject according to the system. E. g. *A list of English tales and prose romances printed before 1740.* By Arundell Esdaile (London, 1912).

There is something to be said for either procedure. The Library of Congress uses a scheme devised more for convenience in finding the bibliography of a desired topic than to show relationship of the sec-tions ; Dewey reproduces the whole system under subject bibliography (016) ; the Newberry Library designates the bibliography of a subject by a lower-case letter, instead of a capital, followed by the number assigned to the subject itself, thus paralleling the system. Theoretically considered, the classing of subject bibliography with the subject itself, e.g. by a subheading at the beginning of the section, seems the most logical ; the student of the subject needs the bibliography as much if not more than he needs other works relating to the subject. Most members of the library staff, however, want bibliography easily accessible and this is not feasible unless it is brought together. Departmental libraries and others having subject departments will class with the subject. Los Angeles and Baltimore do so. Certain topics, however, do not permit of this treatment, e.g. prohibited books, lists of which must of necessity be classed in bibliography.

53 Special collections

Catalogs and lists of books in a collection covering some special subject located in a single library : Class under bibliography of the topic, not with general catalogs of the library. E.g. (1) *Catalog of the Washington collection in the Boston Athenæum* . . . (Boston, 1897). (2) *Revised catalog of the J. Sanford Saltus collection of Louis XVII books in the library of the Salmagundi Club* (New York, 1905).

The author catalog will serve sufficiently as an inventory of the special collections in a given library.

Examples cited are classed : (1) and (2) by L.C. in personal bibliography and by D.C. in bibliography of individuals. Cf. Bibliography of individuals: 48c, note.

54 Auction and booksellers' catalogs

Auction and booksellers' catalogs, when on specific subjects: Class with bibliography of the subject best illustrated by them.

Catalogs of manuscripts. See Manuscripts: 60.

55 Library catalogs

(a) Catalogs of all the books in a public or institutional library: Class under library catalogs according to system. E.g. *Catalogue of the British Museum library.*

(b) Catalogs of books on a special subject in the library: Class in subject bibliography. E.g. *A list of books on the history of science* [in] the John Crerar Library (Chicago, 1911).

(c) Finding-lists of all the books in a library, even when issued in separate volumes covering sections of the whole collection: Class under library catalogs, not under subjects covered by the sections.

The works falling under (b) may be scattered through the classification; those falling under (c) are classed together, and if scattered by subject will defeat the purpose of the finding-list. The author entry will bring all lists together under the name of the library.

56 Libraries, Public

Public or semipublic libraries: Class by geographical division, not by type of library, e.g. college, professional school, municipal.

This is the John Crerar rule. D.C. provides for classing either by type or by geographic division as desired. It is difficult to see what service is rendered, either to readers or to library assistants, by dividing up libraries open to the public according to the institutions with which they are connected; library school libraries, however, prefer arrangement by type.

57 Libraries, Private

(a) Private libraries: Class alphabetically by the names of the owners in the section devoted to private libraries.

unless the type of library is so specialized as to make the contents of the library or its publications valuable for the bibliography of the subject. Cf. 57b.

(b) A catalog of a private library, when that library has been gathered professedly to illustrate the literature of a special subject, or practically and predominantly does so: Class under the bibliography of that special subject. E.g. (1) *Colored book plates and their values; sporting books, works on natural history, travels, etc. . . . collected by William C. Dulles.* Ed. by Francis P. Harper (Princeton, N.J., 1913). Class in bibliography of illustrated books. (2) *The historical library of Dr. George C. F. Williams . . . relating to the American revolution.* (New York, 1926). Class in bibliography of the American revolution.

As such catalogs are usually entered under the name of the owner in the author catalog, there is nothing gained, and often valuable bibliographical material is buried, by classing them along with private libraries of miscellaneous content.

MANUSCRIPTS

58 Original manuscripts

Original manuscripts will usually be kept like rare books in a place by themselves. It is recommended that they be classed by subject rather than alphabetically by authors, except in the case of manuscripts in oriental or other languages known only to specialists. Manuscripts in these less known languages should be classed by language, irrespective of the subject matter. Cf. 256e. A symbol, e.g. MS, prefixed to the call-number, will automatically bring the manuscripts together and yet they will stand in order of the classification.

59 Facsimiles of manuscripts

(a) Facsimiles of manuscripts designed to show the style of writing of different periods, abbreviations, etc. Class in paleography. E.g. Facsimiles of Greek or Roman manuscripts.

(b) Facsimiles of charters and other documents designed

as historical sources: Class in paleography. E.g. *Facsimiles of royal and other charters in the British Museum* (London, 1903–).

The reason for not classing these in history is that only experts in the reading of manuscripts can use them, and hence they will not be used by ordinary readers. The subject catalog must bring out the subject matter of them.

L.C. classes in *documents* (CD105) under diplomatics (History). D.C. classes in history.

(c) Facsimiles of illuminated manuscripts: Class in art. E.g. *Illuminated manuscripts in the British Museum.* By George F. Warner (London, 1903). Students of the art of illumination make frequent use of this type of book.

L.C. classes in *illuminated manuscripts* (ND2897) under art. D.C. classes in book rarities (096.1).

(d) Facsimiles of Biblical manuscripts: Class under the Bible. E.g. *Facsimiles of Biblical manuscripts in the British Museum.* Ed. by Frederic G. Kenyon (London, 1900). Class with the original texts of the Bible, where they will be accessible to Biblical students.

L.C. classes in bibliography of the Bible (Z7771.M3).

(e) Facsimiles of autographs: Class with books on autographs. E.g. *Facsimiles of royal, historical, literary, and other autographs in the British Museum.* Ed. by George F. Warner (London, 1895–99. 5 series).

L.C. classes autographs (Z42) under paleography.

(f) Facsimiles of complete works in manuscript intended for literary or textual study: Class by subject or language. E.g. Facsimiles of Irish manuscripts issued by the Royal Irish Academy. Class in Irish literature.

(g) "Princeps editions" of ancient manuscripts recovered in modern times, especially of the classical authors: Class with the works of these authors, not in paleography. E.g. *Aristotle on the constitution of Athens,* "now for the first time given to the world from the unique text in the British Museum papyrus cxxxi" (London, 1891).

(h) Facsimiles of other single manuscripts: Class by

subject. E.g. Händel's "Messiah," Shelley's "Skylark," the Domesday book.

The New York State Library rule is to class all facsimiles of manuscripts "with the manuscripts themselves," i.e. in 417, "unless the manuscripts themselves would be classed elsewhere," i.e. by subject. This is apparently based on the assumption that users of these facsimiles will use them as manuscripts instead of as texts. The increasing use of the photostat to reproduce manuscripts for use as the original texts of a given work makes the classification of the reproductions by subject more desirable. The catalog will call attention to the presence in the library of the manuscript in facsimile. Genealogical works, for example, whether in handwriting or typewriting, are of no interest as manuscripts; facsimiles of illuminated manuscripts are of great interest under illumination.

L.C. provides for facsimiles of particular manuscripts (Z115Z) under paleography, e.g. *Jenaer liederhandschrift*.

60 Catalogs of manuscripts

Class catalogs of manuscripts in the following order of precedence:

1. Manuscripts on a special subject or in a special form (e.g. illuminated)
2. Manuscripts in the same language
3. Manuscripts existing in a given country, city, or library

E.g. (1) Descriptive list of manuscript collections of the State Historical Society of Wisconsin . . . on American history. Class in bibliography of American history. (2) A list of French manuscripts on the French revolution contained in the Bibliothèque Nationale would go under bibliography of the revolution; one of French manuscripts on many subjects would go under language, not by locality, which will be reserved for those in many languages but preserved in one place or one library.

This rule is invoked in cases where subject, language, or locality might with equal propriety be selected. L.C. subdivides *manuscripts* (Z6601–) under subject bibliography.

61 Manuscripts of individual authors

(a) Catalogs or descriptions of the manuscripts of an individual writer: Class with bibliography of his writings.

(b) Extracts from the manuscripts of a given author: Class by subject like any book.

INCUNABULA

62 Incunabula or works printed before 1500 (or 1550)

This will cover Bibles, works of the church fathers, writings of the Greek or Latin authors, as well as other works; also facsimiles of them. Facsimiles are obviously of the same interest as the originals as specimens of printing. Works of this period rarely have any use as informational literature, and if used as texts at all, are preferred by readers in later editions.

The arrangement of incunabula is largely a concern of the system of classification; but libraries having large collections find useful the arrangement adopted by the British Museum Library: country, city, press, title; the sequence being chronological throughout. By following this comprehensive catalog, moreover, use may be made of the Proctor numbers both to arrange the collection and to refer to the catalog for details.

(a) Original incunabula: Class by themselves under rare printing.

(b) A facsimile of a single work printed in the fifteenth century: Class with incunabula, not by subject. E.g. *The Fifteen O's and other prayers.* Printed . . . by William Caxton. Reproduced in photo-lithography by Stephen Ayling (London, 1869). Class with incunabula, leaving to the catalog to bring it out as an edition of a book otherwise interesting for its contents.

(c) A work treating of a special group of incunabula, e.g. Bibles: Class under bibliography of the subject, not under bibliography of incunabula. E.g. *Fifteenth century Bibles; a study in bibliography.* By Wendell Prime (New York, 1888). Class under bibliography of the Bible.

The reason for this apparent inconsistency is that when grouped by subject, incunabula assume an added interest aside from their connection with printing and become of value for the bibliography or history of the subject. Moreover, incunabula will be arranged by presses with no provision for bringing out their subject matter.

Example cited is classed by L.C. in bibliography of the Bible (Z7770).

(d) Publications of famous early presses like the Froben or Aldine presses: Keep together under rare printing.

As the period covered by these presses includes both the fifteenth and sixteenth centuries, the publications of the same press should be kept together. L.C. classes in individual presses (Z232) only works *on* the printers or their work; D.C. classes the books printed as *rarities* (094.1).

63 Incunabula Bibles

Bibles printed before 1500: Class with incunabula; class here also facsimiles of incunabula Bibles. E.g. 42-Line Bible.

The bibliographical interest in Bibles printed before 1500 outweighs interest in them as texts of the Bible.

64 Prohibited books. Erotica

(a) Works deemed unsuitable for general public use or prohibited, e.g. in the *Index librorum prohibitorum:* Class by subject but shelve, if so desired, in locked cases.

(b) Lists of erotica or of prohibited books: Class in bibliography. E.g. (1) *Index librorum prohibitorum.* (Salmuri, 1601); also in many later editions. (2) *The Roman index of forbidden books explained.* By Francis S. Betten (2d ed.; Chicago, 1932).

L.C. classes lists of prohibited books (Z1019–) in bibliography; D.C. classes them in general bibliography (098.1) but bibliographies of such lists (016.0981) under subject bibliography.

(c) Bibliography of works *on* erotica or *on* prohibited books: Class in subject bibliography.

L.C. classes all bibliography of erotica (Z5865) under subject bibliography; D.C. classes as above rule (016.0981).

BINDINGS

65 Books in extra fine bindings, acquired or kept as specimens of binding or for exhibition

Class together as bindings, not by subject.

The subject catalog will bring out the subject of the book; and as this copy of the work will not ordinarily be used for reading but only for exhibition, its value lies more in its appearance than in its contents.

L.C. does not class together books in notable bindings but only facsimiles of them (Z269); D.C. classes rare bindings (095) under bibliography.

PHILOSOPHY

66 Definition and scope of the class

"Philosophy is the attempt to organize our collective knowledge of the universe into some consistent explanation of the ultimate realities that underlie it. In this broad general sense it is used by our classifications. The philosophy of a special science means an attempt to get at the underlying principles of that particular science and it belongs with the particular science. Much popular literature is in a popular sense 'a philosophy of life'; but in general such unsystematic discussion should be classed in literature, leaving the class philosophy to contain works that formulate the realities of mind and matter in some systematic order, and to the history of the attempts to do so."—(Pettee).

67 Works of philosophers

(a) The collected works of philosophers and criticism of them: Class in the section of philosophy assigned to individual philosophers, not under the system of philosophy or school of thought that they represent or are supposed to represent. E.g. Class Hegel's works under German philosophers, not under idealism.

(b) Individual works written by well-known philosophers upon specific topics in philosophy: Class by topic. E.g. Kant's *Ethics*. Class under ethics. But Hegel's *Logic*, being really a metaphysical treatise laying the foundation for his system of philosophy, is best classed with his collected works.

(c) Treatises of writers not fully recognized as "philosophers": Class by topic unless the treatise is practically a system of philosophy. E.g. *Knowledge, life and reality*. By George T. Ladd (New York, 1909). Class under American philosophers; but class his *Physiological psychology* under psychology.

(d) Views of philosophers upon topics other than philosophic, e.g. education: Class by topic, but in case of doubt,
prefer philosophy. E.g. *The educational theory of Im-
manuel Kant.* Tr. and ed. by Edward Franklin Buchner
(Philadelphia, 1908). Class under pedagogy.

68 Philosophic ideas in literature

Class as literature. E.g. Philosophy of the Meistersingers.

Philosophy in literature is generally more in the nature of a certain outlook on life than a systematic attempt to understand the ultimate reality of the universe.

69 Schools of thought

Reserve this section of philosophy for comprehensive
treatises and history of given schools of thought, e.g. idealism, materialism. Do not class here works written by adherents of a given school upon topics other than philosophic.
E.g. *Die Geschichtsphilosophie Hegel's und der Hegelianer
bis auf Marx und Hartmann.* Von Paul Barth (Leipzig,
1890). Although this work gives the views on the philosophy of history of one group of writers and that group a
school of philosophy, yet the underlying topic is the philosophy of history, which has a place under history.

The connotation of schools of thought is so liable to vary with the
field or the period during which the terms are used, that the classifier
should determine carefully the meaning in which a term is used before
assigning a book to a given heading. The term idealism, for example,
is applied to the philosophy of Plato, to that of Bishop Berkeley, and
to Hegel's, yet the three theories differ widely. Humanism is a term
used for a literary movement of the time of the Renaissance; it is also
a philosophic theory held by some writers of today. Princeton University Library even makes a period division under humanism, dating
the later period from 1900.

Example cited is classed by L.C. in philosophy of history
(D16.8H49).

PSYCHOLOGY

70 Definition and scope of the class

"The science which treats of the mind in any of its aspects."—*(Webster's New international dictionary, 1934).*

Psychology as the science of the soul or of the mind in all of its aspects—nature, origin, destiny, operations, capacities—was formerly always classed in philosophy, where some of the literature treating of it undoubtedly still belongs. Psychology today is largely a field of scientific study concerned with controlled observation of mental states and acts, experiments and tests, or deep-seated causes for human action. "As a definite scientific method of approaching phenomena of all kinds, psychology has the unity that constitutes a distinct class. The psychology of the crowd, the psychology of advertising, the psychology of religion, the psychology of beauty or esthetics, all connote the study of mental phenomena in various aspects."—(Pettee). The question of separating this latter material by the field of study or of keeping it together will be decided by the use to be made of it. Psychology as thus applied is rather a method of inquiry than a body of truth.

Rational psychology treats of the nature of the mind itself or the soul; empirical or experimental psychology studies mental operations without reference to their underlying principle; physiological psychology treats of the relation of the phenomena of consciousness to the nervous system.

71 Psychology as a whole

Works treating comprehensively of the origin, nature and operations of the soul or mind: Class in psychology, under philosophy. E.g. *Psychology*. By Michael Maher, S.J. (Catholic manuals of philosophy, London, 1911).

72 Physiological, empirical, and experimental psychology

Class either in science, if the system provides for them there, or in psychology under philosophy. E.g. (1) *Outlines of physiological psychology*. By George T. Ladd (1890). (2) *Grundzüge der physiologischen psychologie*. Von Wilhelm Wundt (6.aufl.; 1908–11). (3) *Experimental psychology*. By Edward B. Titchener (New York, 1901).

L.C. classes in physiology (QP351–) with alternative in psychology (BF181–) ; D.C. in psychology (159.91) with alternative in physiology (612.821).

73 Social psychology

(a) Psychology of minds in their relations to other minds, e.g. psychology of crowds: Class in sociology.

(b) Folk psychology, the psychology of races, peoples and nations, covering social groups, language, religion and art: Class in race and ethnic *psychology* under philosophy. E.g. *Völkerpsychologie.* Von Wilhelm Wundt (Leipzig, 1900–1914).

(c) Psychic life of primitive peoples: Class in anthropology.

L.C. classes in *psychic life of primitive people* (GN451–) under anthropology; D.C. in *psychology* (159.92241) under philosophy.

74 Educational psychology

Class in education, if system permits. E.g. *Educational psychology.* By Edward Lee Thorndike (New York, 1913–14).

Educational psychology is the application of psychology to education, is a part of educational method, and is written primarily for teachers.

75 Psychology in the sense of psychic causes or principles of special phenomena or events

Class under the topic or event. E.g. (1) *The psychology of revolution.* By Gustave Le Bon; tr. by Bernard Miall (London, 1913). Class under revolution. (2) *An introduction to the experimental psychology of beauty.* By C. W. Valentine (London, rev.ed.; 1919). Class under esthetics. (3) *Narrative technique, a practical course in literary psychology.* By Thomas H. Uzzell (3d. ed.; London, 1934). Class in technique of literary composition. (4) *How to use psychology in business.* By Donald A. Laird (New York, 1936). Class in business method.

The use to be made of books of the character instanced determines the classification. While the student of psychology may and should

make use of such works, their purpose is practical, not theoretic.
Cf. Method vs. Subject-matter: 14.
   Examples cited are classed: (1) by L.C. (DC149) under French
Revolution. (2) by L.C. in *esthetics* (N66) under art.

76 Psychology of politics and history

Class under national character, which covers them both.

77 Psychology of industry—labor, production, distribution, advertising

Class under the theory of that branch of industry concerned, e.g. theory of labor organization, theory of advertising. (John Crerar Library).

ETHICS

78 Professional and business ethics

Works dealing with the ethics of a specific profession or
business: Class under theory of the profession or business.
—(Los Angeles). E.g. (1) *Economics and the ethics of
medicine.* By Bureau of Medical Economics, American
Medical Association (Chicago, 1936). (2) *Professional
ethics.* By J. C. Bayles (n.p., 1886). (3) *Studies in ethics
for nurses.* By Charlotte A. Aikens (Philadelphia, 1923).

Such works are written as a rule for a practical purpose, to inform
professional and business men regarding proper procedure under certain circumstances. They are thus analogous to the works on psychology considered in 75.
   Examples cited are classed: (1) by L.C. in *medical ethics* (R724)
under medicine; by D.C. under ethics (174.2). (2) by L.C. in engineering as a profession (TA157). (3) by L.C. in *nursing ethics*
(RT85) under medicine.

RELIGION

79 Definition and scope of the class

The literature of religion is both philosophic and theological. The philosophic aspects of religion are, in the older literature, considered under so-called natural theology—the rational basis for belief in the existence and providence of God, the future life, the moral life. The scientific method has come to be applied to the study of the different religions of the world, and of ceremonies, cults and practices running through several religions. The distinction between natural and revealed religion, no matter how it may be viewed by writers, is a convenient one for the classifier to use in choosing between philosophy, comparative religions, and theology proper.

80 Theological point of view

(a) Theological doctrines: Class under the topic without reference to the author's point of view. E.g. A work on moral theology written by a Jesuit; one on the Trinity written by a Unitarian; one on Christ written by a Jew. Class under the topic, not with doctrinal works covering respectively the distinctive beliefs of Catholics, Unitarians, or Jews.

This will apply to controversial, systematic or historical treatises upon any individual doctrines of Christianity, e.g. baptism, Lord's Supper, Trinity. It will not apply to individual doctrines or peculiar tenets of Mohammedans, Mormons, Theosophists and the like, because the section theology in most classifications means Christian theology.

(b) Systematic theology: Class under that section, not under the doctrines of the church or sect to which the author belongs, unless the intent of the author is historical and not systematic. E.g. (1) *The "Summa theologica" of St. Thomas Aquinas; literally translated by Fathers of the English Dominican province* (London, 1911–1925). Class in systematic, not in Catholic, theology. (2) *The positive evolution of religion; its moral and social reaction.* By Frederic Harrison (London, 1913). Class under Christianity, not under Positivism, because the work is an examination of the claims of Christianity.

Examples are classed: (1) by L.C. in sources of Catholic doctrines (BX1749). (2) by L.C. in *positivism* (B831) under philosophy.

81 Political opinions of theologians

Class by subject. E.g. *The political theories of Martin Luther.* By L. H. Waring (New York, 1910).

Example cited is classed by L.C. in German political theory (JC141).

82 Sermons

(a) A collection of sermons treating all of one topic: Class under the topic. E.g. (1) *Forefathers' day sermons.* By Charles E. Jefferson (Boston, 1917). Class under Pilgrim Fathers. (2) *Love for the battle-torn peoples; sermon-studies.* By Jenkin Lloyd Jones (Chicago, 1916). Class in addresses and sermons under the European war.

L.C. classes sermons on special topics by subject, but keeps under sermons (BV4255-) such kinds of sermons as e.g. baccalaureate, Christmas, election, marriage, ordination. D.C. classes by subject when the topic is specific, e.g. strikes, but otherwise subdivides by kind and occasion (252.1-) under homiletics.

(b) If this topic is the teaching of a special church: Class in doctrinal theology.

(c) If this topic is a text or book of the Bible: Class under Bible, unless decidedly homiletical in character. E.g. *Sermons on Our Lord's parables.* By C. H. Spurgeon (London, 1894). Class under parables.

"The Union Theological Seminary Library classes sermons by topic always except sermons exegetical of a text of the Bible, thus: (1) Class missionary sermons under missions; (2) funeral or commemorative sermons under biography; (3) dedication or anniversary sermons under social church history; (4) expository sermons, however, not under the text of the Bible treated, but with collections of sermons by the author.

"Within the class sermons: (1) Give language precedence; (2) under language, class by occasion, e.g. Christmas, Fast day, Election, etc."—(Pettee).

CHURCH HISTORY

83 Ecclesiastical districts vs. Geographical districts

(a) A work on the architecture of churches of an ecclesiastical district (diocese, archdeaconry, deanery, parish) or on the secular history or travel in that district: Class under the *geographical* district coterminous with or including the ecclesiastical. E.g. *An architectural survey of the churches in the archdeaconry of Lindisfarne in the county of Northumberland.* By Frederick Richard Wilson (Newcastle-upon-Tyne, 1870). The archdeaconry of Lindisfarne is not coterminous with the island of Lindisfarne, and works upon its church architecture should go under Northumberland, within which it is located.

Example cited is classed by L.C. in religious architecture of Lindisfarne (NA5471.L73).

(b) The history or organization of the ecclesiastical district as such: Class under the church having jurisdiction over it, not under the geographical territory. E.g. *The records of the Northern* [i.e. York (province)] *convocation* (Durham, 1907). Class under Church of England, not under church history of the county of York.

In other words, the history of an ecclesiastical district is more closely linked with the church of which it forms a part than it is with the religious history of the geographical territory within which it lies and where there may coexist several churches or sects.

(c) History of a "parish" meaning a *geographical* division of a county, as in England: Class in secular, not in religious, history, unless professedly church history.

The term "parish" is used in Louisiana to denote a civil division of the state corresponding to a county; in some of the American Colonies the term was formerly used, especially in New England, as synonymous with "town."

84 Local churches

(a) History of an individual church or congregation: Class in local church history, not with history of the denomination. E.g. (1) *One hundred and fiftieth anniversary, First Church of Christ, New Britain, Connecticut, April 25–27, 1908.* Class in church history of New Britain. (2) *Ninetieth anniversary of St. James Church, Chicago, 1834–1924* (Chicago, 1924). (3) *Notre Dame de Chicago, 1887–1937.* [By Pierre J. Peloquin, Chicago, 1937].

L.C. classes Colonial churches in local U.S. *history*. The New York State Library classes in local secular history. Miss Farrar, of the Springfield (Mass.) City Library, recommends this as an alternative. The early New England churches were much more closely identified with the history of the towns than are present churches. Students of the history of a denomination must look in local church history if they expect to cover local affairs of a given denomination.

(b) History of a number of churches of the same denomination, located in the same place, county, or state: Class in history of the denomination. E.g. *List of Congregational ecclesiastical societies established in Connecticut before 1818 with their changes*. Published by the Connecticut Historical Society (Hartford, 1913). Class under Congregationalists.

New York State Library classes history of several churches, when limited to a town or county, in local secular history.

Example cited is classed by L.C. under Congregationalism (BX7148.C8).

85 Medieval church history

Works on the medieval history of the Catholic church in different countries: Class under the church history of the country, not under Catholics in that country, unless the system rules otherwise. Works dealing with the conflicts or diplomatic relations of a country with the Papacy will go there also. E.g. *The medieval church in Scotland*. By John Dowden (Glasgow, 1910). The subject catalog will have, of course, entry under Catholics in Scotland. Cf. Papal relations with countries: 90.

86 Medieval local church history

(a) Class under church history, not under Catholic church in the country or place concerned. E.g. (1) *"Crede mihi"; the most ancient register book of the archbishops of Dublin before the Reformation*. Ed. by J. T. Gilbert (Dublin, 1897). Class in church history of Dublin, not in history of the Catholic church in Ireland. (2) *The register of John Swayne, archbishop of Armagh and primate of Ireland,*

1418–1439. Ed. by D. A. Chart (Belfast, 1935). Class in church history of Armagh.

Example (2) is classed by L.C. in Catholic church in Armagh (BX1507.A7).

Although the local church was, of course, the Catholic church yet its history forms the only church history of the time. This arrangement also keeps together the religious history of the place and avoids committing the library in controversial matters.

"Class all medieval local church history by the local number under general, i.e. secular, history."—(Pettee). To do this, however, seems to sacrifice the subject matter entirely to local considerations.

(b) The medieval history of a town which was also a bishop's see: Class under secular history, unless the intent of the author is to deal only with church affairs. E.g. *Mediaeval Glasgow.* By the Rev. James Primrose (Glasgow, 1913). "Round each of the leading prelates who sat in the chair of St. Kentigern the history of the city during their time has been centered"—(preface). Class in history of Glasgow.

87 Inquisition

Distinguish between three forms of the institution known as the Inquisition: (1) the Inquisition of the Middle Ages; (2) the Inquisition in Spain; (3) the Holy Office or Congregation of the Holy Office in Rome.—*(Catholic encyclopedia).*

The Inquisition is classed by L.C. as a topic (BX1711) in Roman Catholic church under religion; D.C. classes it in persecutions (272.2) under religion, with an alternative for the Spanish Inquisition in history of Spain (946.04) ; Los Angeles classes the Inquisition in Spain, as an institution controlled by the state, in history. An adaptation of the D.C. classification of religion, made for the use of Catholic libraries by August Reyling, O.F.M., puts the whole literature of the Inquisition in church discipline (262.9).

(a) Inquisition of the Middle Ages: Class as topic under history of the Catholic church. E.g. (1) *The Inquisition.* By G. G. Coulton (London, 1929). (2) *The story of the Inquisition.* (New York, 1928).

(b) Spanish Inquisition: Class as a subdivision under history of the Inquisition. E.g. (1) *Auto de fe celebrado en la ciudad de Logroño, 1610.* [By the Inquisition—Spain.] (Madrid, 1820). (2) *Torquemada and the Spanish Inquisition.* By Rafael Sabatini (Boston, 1924).

(c) Holy Office in Rome: Class as a topic under the polity or system of government of the Catholic church.

88 Chronicles, Monastic

Class under history of the country and period with which they are concerned, unless concerned avowedly with the history of a monastery or of a monastic order. E.g. Ingulph's *Chronicle of the abbey of Croyland with continuations* (London, 1854). Class with other chronicles of England A.D. 704–1486.

The monastic chroniclers were the principal historians of the times in which they lived.

Example cited is classed by L.C. in history of Croyland, England. (DA690.C79).

89 Denominational periodicals

Periodicals issued by members or organizations of a given church or denomination, and distinctively marked as to their scope: Class by professed scope. E.g. (1) *Mid-America, an Historical Review* (formerly the *Illinois Catholic Historical Review*) Chicago, 1918- . Class in history of the West, not in Catholic church in Illinois, because it deals with history, both secular and religious, of Catholics in the mid West region. (2) *Catholic Historical Review* (Catholic University of America, Washington, D.C.). Class in general historical periodicals, not under Catholic church. (3) *Catholic World* (New York). Class in general periodicals.

This is in accord with the rule to class a book on theology by its subject and not by the point of view of the author. A denominational periodical will naturally stress the aspect of the subject peculiar to the denomination.

90 Papal relations with countries

(a) A collection of papal letters or documents relating to a country: Class under the church history of that country, not under its general or secular history. E.g. *Calendar of entries in the papal registers relating to Great Britain and Ireland; papal letters.* Pub. by the Master of the Rolls (v.1, 1198+; London, 1893+). Class under medieval church history of Great Britain.

While such documents are often closely connected with secular or diplomatic history, the justification of the rule is found in the fact that the ground of all relations between the government of a country and the See of Rome has been primarily the Catholic church in that country and its relations to the state.

Example cited is classed by L.C. in *sources* (DA25) under *history* of England.

(b) Papal letters or documents relating to a special topic or event: Class by topic. E.g. (1) *Bullarium Ordinis ff. minorum s.p. Francisci Capucinorum.* A Michaele a Tugio (Romæ, 1740–52. 7v.). Class under Capuchins. (2) Bull of demarcation of Alexander VI. Class in Spanish discoveries in America.

(c) Works on relation or dealings of a nation with the papacy: Class in church history of the country concerned, unless the matter is strictly secular history. E.g. *L'église romaine et le premier empire, 1800–1814.* Par le comte d'Haussonville (Paris, 1870. 5v.). Class in church history of France.

While the medieval relation of emperor or king with the pope was often broader than ecclesiastical, yet the *primary* concern of the papacy was the church in a given country, not political affairs merely as such. Hence it is difficult to draw the line between ecclesiastical and secular history. L.C. subdivides papal relations with countries by country (BX1197–, 1260–, etc.) under history of the Roman Catholic church.

COMPARATIVE RELIGION

91 Change of religion

A work treating of the passage of a people or nation from one religion to another: Class under the later religion. E.g. *Paganism and Christianity in Egypt.* By Philip David Scott-Moncrieff (Cambridge, 1913). Class under Christianity in Egypt.

The reasons for this are: (1) the later religion is the one that in this case prevails and hence is the more important; (2) the origin of a new movement is more often important to the student than the decay of an old one.

92 Race or religion vs. Topic

A work on the part taken by a race (e.g. Jews) or by members of a church (e.g. Catholics) in a given movement: Class under the topic, subdivided if desired, in preference to history of the race or church. E.g. (1) *The importance of the Jews for the preservation and revival of learning during the middle ages.* By Dr. M. I. Schleiden; tr. by Maurice Kleimenhagen (London, 1911). Class under literary history of the Middle Ages. (2) *Catholic churchmen in science.* By James J. Walsh (Philadelphia, 1906–09. 2 series). Class in biography of scientists.

Examples cited are classed: (1) by L.C. in medieval history of the Jews (DS124). (2) by L.C. in biography of scientists (Q141).

93 Religious doctrines and practices

(a) A distinctively Christian doctrine: Class by topic in doctrinal theology. E.g. *The idea of atonement in Christian theology.* By Hastings Rashdall (London, 1919).

(b) A single doctrine or practice, e.g. divination, or sacrifice, as believed or practiced in a non-Christian religion: Class under the religion. E.g. *Greek divination.* By W. R. Halliday (London, 1913). Class under Greek religion.

Example cited is classed by L.C. in *Greek divination* (BF1765) under occult sciences (philosophy).

(c) A religious belief or practice running through several religions, e.g. sacrifice, or nature worship, treated comparatively: Class by topic in comparative religion. E.g. *The ideals of asceticism, an essay in the comparative study of religion.* By Oscar Hardman (London, 1924). Class under asceticism as a topic in comparative religion.

The alternative of detaching and segregating under a separate heading religious doctrines or practices of every kind is decidedly "advanced," and is even repellent to many minds. Thus to put under one heading Jewish, Christian, Roman (pagan), and heathen sacri-

fice may seem logical to some students of comparative religion; but
it will not fit the older literature.

"I should class all religious rites and practices strictly under the
religion of which they form a part."—(Pettee).

94 Animals in folk-lore and religions

Class in folk-lore. E.g. *The place of animals in human
thought.* By the Countess Evelyn Martinengo Cesaresco
(London, 1909). Class in folk-lore.

L.C. classes *animals* as a topic (BL439–) under comparative
mythology; but the example is classed in *souls of animals* (BD428)
under metaphysics.

Animal lore will usually be classed in folk-lore; emblematic treatment of animals in Christian symbolism or in comparative religion.
Cf. Animals in art: 228.

SOCIOLOGY

95 Definition and scope of class

Social sciences is a heading used by Cutter in his classification to cover economics, sociology (in a narrow sense),
political science and law. Dewey uses the term sociology to
cover the same fields. Library of Congress excludes political science and law from the field of social sciences.

As a class without subdivision sociology or the social
sciences will be used by the classifier mostly for periodicals
and for cyclopedias and comprehensive works.

96 Economic, legal or political documents

(a) A collection of economic, legal or political documents, brought together to illustrate, or as source material
for, economic, legal or political history respectively: Class
by subject covered.

(b) Such documents, when brought together to illustrate,
or as source material for, the history of a given country or
period: Class in history of the country or period. E.g.
*Constitutions and other select documents illustrative of the
history of France, 1789–1907.* By F. W. Anderson (Minne-
apolis, 1908). Class in history of France.

The subject catalog will always bring out, under "sources of history," material of value; while the student of the history of economics or of legal history has quite as much right as has the historian to find economic sources under economics and legal source material under law. Cf. Illustrative material: 13.

97 Statistics

(a) Works of statistics of population, giving figures only: Class in statistics, by locality. E.g. (1) *Statistics of the United States in 1860* (Washington, 1866). (2) *Topical index of population census reports, 1900–1930* (Ann Arbor, Mich., 1934). (3) *Census of Great Britain, 1851* (London, 1852).

(b) Lists of names of families or of individuals recorded in census reports: Class in local history or genealogy. E.g. (1) *Heads of families in Worcester county, Maryland, at the first census, 1790* (Washington, 1931). (2) *Heads of families at the first census* (Washington, 1908?).

L.C. classes national lists in census, local in history; D.C. classes in genealogy.

(c) Statistics of special topics: Class by topic, dividing by country or place when treated locally. E.g. (1) *International yearbook of agricultural statistics, 1910* (Rome). (2) *Statistics for beginners in education.* By Frederick Lamson Whitney (New York, 1929). (3) *A work and study book of statistical methods used in education.* By Henry A. Cross (Ann Arbor, Mich., 1933).

D.C. provides a form division (00031) for statistics under any subject.

Libraries using the Government classification of federal documents will keep statistical documents under the issuing office. Los Angeles puts second copies only with the topic.

(d) Mathematical theory of statistics. See Mathematical theory of statistics: 178.

(e) A work treating of statistics bearing on two subjects: Determine the relation of the two subjects as treated in the book and class by 15.

Statistics of education and psychology, for example, may be covered by educational psychology.

POLITICAL SCIENCE

98 Administration, constitutions and institutions

Administration for the classifier covers operations of the government and of its officials; constitutions, constitutional law and history cover written and unwritten fundamental structure and law of the state, its interpretation and history; institutions cover political, religious, educational, and social organizations. Politics is distinguished from history. History is the record of events, including their causes or the circumstances under which they occur; politics is the discussion of contemporary measures, policies, or theories, including the sources or data upon which such contemporary opinion is based. History is written after the events narrated; politics are written while the events are occurring. History of the discussions is either bibliography or politico-literary history.

99 Fascism

Fascism is the term devised to express the policies and the form of government established by the Fascisti, "an Italian organization originated by loyal patriots to oppose all radical elements in the country, as Bolshevists, Communists and the like."—(*Webster's New international dictionary,* 1934). L.C. classes fascism under forms of government (JC481); D.C. in state socialism (335.6) unless governmental aspect is emphasized.

(a) Theoretical works on fascism: Class in political theory. E.g. (1) *The philosophy of fascism.* By Mario Palmieri (Chicago, 1936). (2) *Fascism and social revolution.* By R. Palme Dutt (New York, 1934).

(b) Works dealing with events leading up to or following the establishment of fascism in a country: Class in history of the country. E.g. (1) *El fascismo, su origen, organización, doctrina, lucha y triunfo de Mussolini en Italia, 1919–1922.* [By] N. Cebreiros [Madrid, 1933]. (2) *Fascism—make or break? German experience.* By R. Braun;

tr. by M. Davidson (London, 1935). (3) *Spain in revolt.*
By Harry Gennes and Theodore Repard (New York, 1936).

Examples cited are classed by both L.C. and D.C. in recent history of the countries named.

(c) Works on fascism in Italy: Class according to the scope of the book, whether treating of the government as a whole or of some special topic. E.g. (1) *The new fascist state, a study of Italy under Mussolini.* By Edwin Hare Hullinger (New York, 1928). (2) *The structure of the corporate state.* Tr. by Anna Waring (London, 1933).

As the fascist government in Italy controls all large forms of activity in the state, works on fascism are likely to treat of a variety of topics. Fascism is a mode of administration applied to economic, social and political conditions and activities; the subject catalog may better be used to meet a demand, that may be only a passing one, for special applications of fascism.

Example cited is classed: (2) by L.C. in *industry and state* (HD3616.I83); by D.C. in state socialism (335.6).

(d) Works on fascism as a form of government in a particular country: Class with works on the government of that country.

The D.C. editors write: "We should class with other works on the present form of government of that country, either in history or constitutional law." As fascism has not yet (1939) been established under quite the same form in any other country than Italy, the works treating of it elsewhere are largely movements, propaganda, or events, and thus fall under (b) above.

(e) Economic foundations of fascism: Class under fascism. E.g. *The economic foundation of fascism.* By Paul Einzig (London, 1934).

Example cited is classed by Queens Borough in economics of Italy.

(f) Influence of fascism on social, industrial, or technical activities: Class under the activity, e.g. aviation. E.g. *Fascismo ed aviazione.* [By] Attilio Longoni (Milano [1931]).

As this is a case of one factor influencing another, it falls under 15b.

Example cited is classed by L.C. in aeronautics (TL526.I8); so also by D.C. (629.130945). Franklin and Marshall C. keeps together all of the literature on fascism.

100 Nazi régime. Hitlerism

The Nazis are members of the Nationalsozialistische Partei in Germany. Hitlerism is "the extreme nationalistic doctrines of the National Socialistic party under the leadership of Adolf Hitler, from about 1930."—(*Webster's New international dictionary*, 1934).

(a) Works on the Nazi régime in Germany, treating of nazism as a form of political government: Class in political theory. E.g. *Principii politici del nazionalsocialismo.* [By] Carl Schmitt (Firenze, 1935).

(b) Works on political events in Germany during the Nazi period: Class in history of Germany. E.g. *Zur geschichte des nationalsozialismus.* Von Walter Frank (Hamburg, 1934). (2) *Swastika over Germany.* By Siegfried Lipschitz (New York, 1933).

101 History of the political theory of a special country or school.

Class under history of political science, not under politics and government of the country, unless the intent of the book is primarily descriptive of institutions and not of ideas. E.g. *The political ideas of the Greeks.* By J. L. Myres (London, 1927). Class in history of political theory.

102 National political ideals

(a) Works on national ideals: Class by the feature of national life concerned. E.g. Class Bonapartism under French constitution and government, as it concerns the fundamental organization of the French state; Monroe doctrine under American foreign relations, as it concerns the relations of America to foreign nations.

(b) Works on certain ideals or principles, e.g. pacifism, theocracy, as exemplified in the history of a given nation or community: Class in history of the nation or community. E.g. (1) *Peace principles exemplified in the early history of Pennsylvania.* By Samuel M. Janney (Philadelphia, 1888). Class under history of Pennsylvania. (2) *Wonder-working*

providence of Zion's Saviour in New England. By Captain
Edward Johnson (London, 1654). Class in Colonial history of Massachusetts.

103 Government documents

(a) "When indefinite in scope, or composed of bound
volumes of various departmental reports, or when purely
administrative in character: Class geographically under
administration."—(John Crerar Library). E.g. U.S. Department of the Interior, *Report.*

(b) "When limited to a special subject: Class under subject."—(John Crerar Library). E.g. Illinois Tax Commission, *Report;* U.S. Office of Education, *Reports.*

Libraries using the Government classification of United States
public documents will, of course, keep all publications of the same department or bureau shelved together. This arrangement has much to
recommend it as a labor-saver, since call-numbers are assigned in
Washington to the thousands of government documents distributed
by the Superintendent of Documents. Cards referring to these Government numbers may be filed under subjects in the subject catalog.
Printed indexes to government documents are practically supplements
to the catalog of any library having extensive collections of documents and should be shelved accordingly.

104 Political policy

History of the political policy of a country toward a dependency of that country: Class under the politics of the
dependency. E.g. *Gladstone and Ireland; the Irish policy
of Parliament from 1850–1894.* By Lord Eversley (London). Class in politics of Ireland.

Such a work is not a history of the dependency because the events
described take place as much in the mother country as in the dependency; neither is it a history of the mother country. Hence the
politics of the dependency, which is the country affected, is the subject of the work.

105 Elections

(a) Works dealing with the theory of suffrage and elections: Class under suffrage. E.g. (1) *Reports respecting
the qualifications for the parliamentary franchise in foreign*

countries. By the Foreign Office (London, 1883). *(2) The
presidential primary.* By Louis Overacker (New York,
1926).

L.C. classes election of the *president* (JK521-) under administration.

(b) Campaign literature: Class with political parties;
or, if dealing with current history, in history. E.g. (1) Official reports of the proceedings of the Republican national
conventions. (2) Campaign books. *(3) American ideals
versus the New Deal.* By H. C. Hoover (New York, 1936).
Cf. Politics: 303.

106 Emigration and immigration

(a) Works treating of emigration from one country to
another: Class under *immigration* to the country reached.

(b) Works treating of emigration from one country to
several other countries: Class under *emigration* from the
country of origin. E.g. *A history of emigration from the
United Kingdom to North America, 1763-1912.* By Stan-
ley C. Johnson (London, 1913). Class in emigration from
Great Britain.

(c) Works on immigrants who were the first settlers or
colonists in a local community: Class in local history.—(Los
Angeles). E.g. (1) *The first settlers of Totawa, now Pat-
terson, New Jersey.* By Parke Godwin (New York, 1892).
(2) Early Virginia immigrants. By G. C. Greer (Rich-
mond, 1912).

Colonists in the sense of the first settlers in a locality are to be distinguished by the classifier from immigrants who arrive after such a
settlement has been formed, or who enter a settled country.

INTERNATIONAL RELATIONS

Differences affecting classification between works on international
relations and those on international law are discussed under 127.

107 Foreign relations

(a) Diplomatic relations of two countries: Class under
the country represented or expressed in the point of view

of the author. In the case of official publications, class always under the country issuing the publication. E.g. *American-Japanese relations, an inside view of Japan's policies and purposes.* By Kiyoshi K. Kawakami (New York, 1914). Class under Japan.

The order of names on the title-page is not a guide to the classification.

(b) Diplomatic correspondence respecting a special point, industry, or place: Class under the topic concerned. E.g. (1) *The British case in French Congo.* By Edmund D. Morel (London, 1903). Class under French Congo. (2) *The Panama Canal conflict between Great Britain and the United States of America; a study.* By L. Oppenheim (Cambridge, 1913). Class under Panama Canal (Economics).

(c) Diplomatic correspondence relating to a war. See Diplomatic history of wars: 111.

(d) Claims of one country against another: Class either in international relations or in public finance, according to system, making the country against which the claim is brought the basis of the division by country.

The question of choosing between the claimant or the defendant country is evenly balanced; both countries are interested in the case and both are affected by the outcome. The Queens Borough rule is: "For claims against the U.S., use 336 [public finance] dividing by the number for the country making the claim." An alternative would be to follow the procedure of (a) above.

108 Annexations and unions

(a) Unions of one state, country or town with another state, country or town: Class under the territory absorbed. E.g. *The union of England and Scotland.* By James Mackinnon (London, 1896). Class in history of Scotland.

The reasons are: (1) Such events mark the closing period in the history of the lesser territory; (2) the union concerns more intimately the territory absorbed than the other.

(b) Works on a country that has once been independent but is now absorbed into a larger political division: Class under its own name. E.g. Aragon, Austria.

Histories of the kingdom of Aragon, of Castile, of Navarre, while
properly given separate sections in the history of Spain, are not strictly
local works. So history of Northumbria, one of the Anglo-Saxon
kingdoms, goes properly in Saxon England.

109 Boundary disputes and arbitration

Cases, counter claims, arguments, and decisions regarding
territories in dispute between two countries: Class with
works on boundaries of the country in possession of the territory at the beginning of the dispute. E.g. The Tacna-
Arica dispute between Chile and Peru. Class under Chile.
If possession is in doubt, class finally under the country that
obtains the territory.

110 Diplomatic correspondence and memoirs of diplomats

(a) When personal and descriptive of events: Class
under the history of the country described, even though the
author be the ambassador of another country. E.g. *Recollections of a minister* [from the United States] *to France,
1869–1877.* By E. B. Washburne (London, 1887. 2v.).
Class in French history.

(b) When official: Class in foreign relations of the
country represented. E.g. *Correspondence diplomatique de
Talleyrand; ambassade de Talleyrand à Londres, 1830–
1834* (Paris, 1891–   ). Class in French foreign relations.

Example cited is classed by L.C. in political history of France
(DC266.5).

111 Diplomatic history of wars

(a) Diplomatic history or documentary material of a
war: Class under the history of that war, rather than with
the other diplomatic history of the country. E.g. *The revo-
lutionary diplomatic correspondence of the United States.*
Ed. by Francis Wharton (Washington, 1889. 6v.). Class
under American revolution.

(b) Diplomatic relations of two countries, either before
or following a war between them: Class under the history
of this war if the intent of the author is to illustrate the causes
or the effect of the war. E.g. *The Turco-Italian war and its*

problems. By Sir Thomas Barclay (London, 1912). "The object is . . . to place the questions arising out of the war . . . before the reader"—(preface) ; the matter is all diplomatic. Class under history of Tripoli.

This is in line with the usual practice of systems in grouping various aspects of a war around its history. Otherwise treat like other diplomatic history of the country concerned.

Diplomatic relations. See Foreign relations : 107.

112 Foreign intervention

A work dealing with the intervention of one country in the affairs of another : Class under the history of the latter, not under foreign relations of the intervening country. E.g. *Cuba and the intervention* [by the United States]. By Albert G. Robinson (London, 1905). Class under history of Cuba.

Diplomatic relations may be considered to stop where intervention or occupation begins.

113 Influence of one country upon another

Class under the country influenced. E.g. *Scotland and the French revolution*. By Henry W. Meikle (Glasgow, 1912). A "study of the influence of the French Revolution on Scotland." Class under history of Scotland.

114 Origin of political institutions

Institutions of one country compared with those of another, to show derivation : Class under the country whose institutions have been derived. E.g. English common law as the source of New England institutions. Class under New England governments.

The purpose of such a book is to illustrate the history of the country deriving its institutions, not the country furnishing the model.

LEGISLATION

115 Legislation and legislative bodies

(a) The decrees of royal councils and governing bodies, especially those vested with administrative and judicial, as

well as legislative, powers : Class, on account of their comprehensive character, in history, not in legislation. E.g.
*Jugements et délibérations du conseil souverain de la Nou-
velle-France* (Quebec, 1885–91. 6v.). Class in history of
Canada.

(b) History of legislative bodies (e.g. Parliament, Congress) : Class in group by itself, not with general constitutional history of the country. E.g. *The high court of parliament and its supremacy.* By Charles Howard McIlwain
(New Haven, 1910). Class with history of Parliament.

The legislative bodies of a country form only *one* feature of its
constitution and works on them are better kept apart from more general constitutional works.

Example cited is classed by L.C. in *juridical powers* of Parliament
(JN557) under constitutional history of Great Britain.

(c) Mode of election and history of elections to a legislative body, e.g. Congress, Parliament: Class as topic
under that body. E.g. (1) *The election of senators* [to
Congress]. By George H. Haynes (New York, 1906).
(2) Contested election cases.

L.C. classes elections to the senate (JK1175–   ) and to the house
(JK1351–   ) under constitutional history of those bodies; D.C.
classes contested elections in suffrage (324.277) and *election to legislative bodies* (328.335) under legislation.

(d) History of individual bills, e.g. the Reform Bill of
1832 : Class by the topic.

POLITICAL PARTIES

116 Political parties

The history of political parties in a single state or city:
Class with local, not with national politics. E.g. *History of
the republican party in Illinois, 1854–1912.* By Charles A.
Church (Rockford, 1912). Class under Illinois politics,
although state parties undoubtedly have close affiliation with
the national organization.

L.C. subdivides national parties by states (JK2301–   ) under constitutional history of the U.S.

117 "Liberal" and "Conservative"

When the terms "liberal" and "conservative" connote not a party but a tendency of thought or a movement: Class by topic. E.g. (1) *Liberal Christianity.* By Jean Reville (London, 1903). Class under doctrinal theology in general, not under sects. (2) *Conservatism.* By Lord H. Cecil (London, 1912). (3) *Liberalism.* By L. T. Hobhouse (London, 1912). Class under public opinion.

ECONOMICS

118 Economic planning

(a) Comprehensive works on state or national planning: Class in economic policy or conditions. E.g. (1) *Economic planning.* [By] G. D. H. Cole (New York, 1935). (2) *NRA economic planning.* By Charles Frederick Roos (Bloomington, Ind., 1937).

Examples cited are classed: (1) by L.C. in economic policy (HC256.3); by D.C. in economics (330.942). (2) by L.C. in industry and state (HD3616.U46); by D.C. in economic organization (338.0973).

(b) Works on planning along special lines, e.g. city planning, conservation of natural resources, preservation of wild life: Class under the matter immediately concerned, e.g. the resources to be conserved, the end to be attained. E.g. (1) *City planning; housing.* By Werner Hegemann (New York, 1936). (2) *State planning, programs and accomplishments.* [By] National Resources Committee (Washington, 1937). (3) *Wildlife conservation.* Report of Special Committee . . . (Washington, 1937). (4) *Economic planning and national defense.* [By James H. B. Bogman] (Washington, 1933).

L.C. classes esthetics of cities (NA9000–   ) under architecture, but provides for civic art and improvement (JS93– , 341– , etc.) under local government. D.C. classes city planning (711) under landscape gardening, but planning of individual cities (914–   ) under description.

The alternative is to bring together works on such planning accord-

ing to the civic agency appointed to carry them out, whether municipal, state, or federal. The question as to who should carry out the
plans, however, is of interest rather to the politician than to the student of the subject. When the publication is official, the author catalog will bring out the agency.

Examples cited are classed: (1) by L.C. in *city planning*
(NA9030) under architecture; by D.C. in *city planning* (711) under
landscape gardening. (2) by L.C. in economic conditions (HC106.3) ;
so also by D.C. (330.973). (3) by L.C. in conservation of wild life
(SK361) ; by D.C. in fishing and hunting (799.0973). (4) by L.C. in
national defense (UA23) ; so also by D.C. (355.210973).

119 Colonial policy

The commercial policy of a country toward her colonies :
Class under the commerce of the mother country, even if but
one colony is concerned. E.g. *Colbert's West India policy.*
By Stewart L. Mims (New Haven, 1912). Class under
commerce of France with the West Indies.

The reasons for this are : (1) the policy is that of the mother country, not that of the colony, however the latter may be affected by it ;
(2) the conditions are common to both ; (3) the point of view is
usually that of the mother country. The reason against it is : the
commercial history of the colony as such is buried in that of the
mother country. But the latter objection is obviated by subdividing
the commerce of the mother country with other countries.

120 Physiology and psychology of labor and of muscular exercise

The conditions best adapted for efficient work by the human or-
ganism form the subject of works on the physiology and psychology
of labor. These studies have for their end the attainment of economic
efficiency ; only incidentally are they contributions to physiology or
to psychology.

(a) Works on the physiology of labor in general : Class
in industrial efficiency. (1) *Organisation physiologique du
travail.* Par Jules Amar (Paris, 1917). (2) *Psychology in
business and industry, an introduction to psychotechnology.*
By John G. Jenkins (New York, 1935).

(b) When more than one activity forms the subject of
the study : Class in physiology or in psychology, according
to aspect.—(John Crerar Library). E.g. *Arbeitsphysiolo-*

gie, zeitschrift, für die physiologie des menschen bei arbeit und sport (Berlin, 1929–). (2) *Effect of physical training on blood volume, hemoglobin, alkali reserve, and osmotic resistance to erythrocytes.* By John Emerson Davis (Chicago, 1936). (3) *Physiology of muscular activity.* By Edward C. Schneider (Philadelphia, 1933).

L.C. classes physiology of exercise (QP301) under physiology. "D.C. classes hygiene of laboring conditions with labor in 331; studies of labor efficiency from the point of view of production management in 658.01 or 658.5."—(D.C. editors).

Cf. Sport medicine: 199.

121 Modeling (Display of garments)

(a) Works on modeling in the sense of displaying garments on the human figure, whether by man or woman: Class in clothing industry. E.g. *Modeling for money, how to become a successful mannequin.* By Carol Lynn (New York, 1937).

D.C. editors write: "in relation to manufacturing 687; fashion modeling 646.01; sales methods 658.855; advertising methods 659.1." Cincinnati classes modeling [by women] in occupations for women, following the topics in L.C.'s HD6073; but this overlooks modeling by men or separates the two.

(b) Works on fashion drawing and dress design: Class by topic under clothing industry. E.g. (1) *Fashion drawing and dress design.* By Mabel Lillian Hall (London, 1928). (2) *Fashion drawing technique.* [By Mabel Lillian Hall] (London, 1933).

L.C. classes in *drawing* (TT509) under dressmaking; D.C. in *drawing* (741) under fine arts.

122 Land owners

Lists of householders and maps showing plots of land, homesteads, farms and the like, of early settlers in a place: Class in local history. E.g. *Owners and occupants of the lots, houses and shops in the town of Providence, R.I. in 1798.* By Henry P. Chace (Providence, R.I., 1914). Class in history of Providence.

123 Communism

Communism has been defined as the common ownership of both industry and its products. It may be practiced voluntarily by a small community living together a common life; it may be advocated as a mode of economic life for nations and even for all mankind; or it may become the basis of a country's government having ramifications far wider than economic conditions. The subject has expanded beyond the bounds that classification can control. The subject catalog may, if desired, bring together the cards of all works treating of communism in any of its aspects.

(a) Works on communism as a theory of economic life: Class in economics. E.g. (1) *The philosophy of communism.* By John Macmurray (London, 1933). (2) *Communism and a changing civilisation.* By Ralph Fox (London, 1935). (3) *El comunismo en España.* [By] E. Matorras (Madrid, 1935).

(b) Works on communism as a form of political government: Class under government.

This rule might be combined with the preceding and made to read: Class according to the trend of the book. This is the practice of the Library of Congress, John Crerar Library, Decimal classification, and others. The older literature was largely economic in trend.

(c) Works advocating communism as both economic and political: Class in economics. E.g. (1) *The communist answer to the world's needs, discussion in economic, political, and social philosophy.* By Julius F. Hecker (London, 1935). (2) *Forward from liberalism.* [By] Stephen Spender (New York, 1937).

(d) Works dealing with history of events leading to establishment of communism in a nation, or descriptive of it as a form of government in a particular country: Class in history of the country. E.g. (1) *Outline history of the Communist party of the Soviet Union.* [By] N. N. Popov (New York, 1934. 2v.). (2) *The Russian Soviet republic.* By Edward Alsworth Ross (New York, 1923). (3) *Soviet communism.* By Sidney and Beatrice Webb (London, 1935).

Examples cited are classed: (1) by L.C. in history of Russia (DK63); by D.C. in history of communism in Russia (335.40947). (2) and (3) by L.C. and D.C. in history of Russia.

124 Finance

(a) Works upon special features of public finance, e.g. monopolies, income tax, in a special country: Class under the topic.

(b) Works upon taxation in a special country or state, or on local taxation: Class in the geographical division under public finance, not under taxation.

D.C. classes local taxation under administration (352.1); other geographic divisions under taxation (336.2). L.C. classes only local taxation directly under local finance (HJ9000–).

(c) Serial publications (annual reports, bulletins) on finance covering only a special state, or treating only of taxation in a given state: Class with other works on local finance, not with periodicals under finance in general or under the heading taxation. E.g. Annual report of the Tax Commission of Illinois. Class under Illinois finance. "A manual of taxation for use in Illinois would be shelved under taxation (336.2)."—(John Crerar Library).

The John Crerar Library rule is: "Under public finance, favor the special subject discussed instead of the locality, as: state monopolies in France, income tax in Illinois, public securities of U.S.A. However, in case of reports and other serial publications of a country or state covering the topic taxation, it seems desirable to class under the geographical division for the country under the general subject of public finance."

(d) Methods of raising revenue for a specific purpose: Class under the topic treated. E.g. *Modern wars and war taxes, a manual of military finance.* By W. R. Lawson (Edinburgh and London, 1912). Class in military art, not in economics, unless military finance is made a subdivision of finance.

The New York State Library classes always in finance. D.C. usually does so.

L.C. classes cost of armaments as topic (UA17) under military art, with alternative (HJ7499) under finance.

LAW

125 Law of special subjects

Law of special subjects, e.g. insurance: Class by subject.
—(John Crerar Library).

Law libraries will have their own special disposition of the law of special subjects, best suited to their functions and needs, but it is doubtful whether any other type of library will subdivide law according to the subject concerned.

126 Legal procedure

Distinguish law from legal procedure, i.e. statutes defining crimes as distinguished from law prescribing the court procedure in dealing with crimes.

INTERNATIONAL LAW

127 International law

International law is defined as "the system of rules that civilized nations acknowledge to be obligatory as their common law for regulating their common rights and duties in peace and war."—*(New standard dictionary)*. International law for the classifier concerns what *ought* or *ought not* to be done in certain situations in which nations may be placed or are involved. It thus differs for the classifier from international relations, which concern what *has* been done or what is *proposed* to be done in given situations. Cf. Foreign relations: 107.

(a) Works discussing what *ought* or *ought not* to be done in certain situations in which nations may be involved: Class in international law. E.g. (1) *International law*. By Charles G. Fenwick (2d ed.; New York, 1934). (2) *A treatise on international law*. By William Howard Hall (8th ed.; Oxford, 1924).

(b) Works discussing or relating what *has* been done or what is *proposed* to be done in given situations: Class in international relations or by topic. E.g. (1) *A history of American foreign policy*. By John Holladay Latané. Rev.

by D. W. Wainhouse (Garden City, 1934). (2) *The international law and diplomacy of the Russo-Japanese War.* By Amos S. Hershey (London, 1906).

Examples cited are classed: (1) by L.C. in U.S. foreign relations (JX1407); so also by D.C. (327.73). (2) by L.C. as topic in foreign relations of the 20th century (JX1393.R8).

(c) Works in which some principle or principles of international law are illustrated or supported by citation of events or of national policies: Class in international law by the topic involved. E.g. (1) *Intervención—conciliación— arbitraje, en las conferencias de la Habana, 1928 y Wáshington, 1929.* [By] Victor M. Maúrtua (Habana, 1929?). (2) *La doctrine de Draco.* Par H. A. Moulin (Paris, 1907). (3) *La Suisse et le droit de libre navigation sur les fleuves internationaux.* By J. Vallotton (Lausanne, 1914).

Examples cited are classed: (1) by L.C. in foreign relations of the American republics (JX1404); by D.C. in arbitration (341.6). (2) by L.C. as topic (JX1393.D8) under international law; by D.C. in international law (341). (3) by L.C. in international rivers (JX4150).

128 International congresses upon special subjects

International congresses upon special subjects, whether diplomatic or professional (technical, etc.) : Class under subject. E.g. Monetary congresses; Limitation of armament; International mining congress.

The John Crerar Library rule is: "Both *diplomatic* congresses, as e.g. The Monetary congress, and also *non-diplomatic,* as e.g. International mining congress, relating to a special subject go with that subject, (respectively, 332.44 and 622.06). Diplomatic congresses of a general nature, and permanent bodies for settling international relations go under International law and relations, 341.1."

129 Treaties

(a) Collections of treaties between two or more countries: Subdivide by country arranging "according to the most important country."—(Dewey).

(b) Treaties relating to a specific subject: Class under the subject.

(c) Commercial treaties: Class under commerce arranging "according to the most important country."— (Dewey).

Treaties signed at the termination of a war will be classed, in general libraries, under the history of that war.

130 Treaty outcomes

Works dealing with the political or economic results of treaties: Class with the subject concerned.—(Los Angeles). E.g. (1) *Mandates; questions of military recruiting, state domain and liquor traffic.* By League of Nations [Geneva, 1926]. (2) *Le mandat sur la Palestine.* [By] Abraham Baumkoller (Paris, 1931). (3) *Protection of minorities in Esthonia.* By League of Nations [Geneva, 1923]. (4) *Reparations, 1932–1933, final report.* By the Canadian Royal Commission . . . (Ottawa, 1933). (5) *Economic consequences of the peace.* By J. M. Keynes (New York, 1920).

Examples cited are classed: (1) by L.C. in the series (League of Nations, Documents). (2) by L.C. (D651.P3) under European war; by D.C. (956.9) under history of Palestine. (3) by L.C. (D651.E8) under European war; by D.C. in internal relations in Palestine (323.1474). (4) by L.C. (D649.C2) under European war; so also by D.C. (940.31422). (5) by L.C. (HC57) under economic history; by D.C. in economic effects of the war (940.314833).

CONSTITUTIONAL LAW AND HISTORY

131 Constitutional conventions, State

(a) Conventions convened by a state for the purpose of ratifying the federal constitution: Class under U.S. constitutional history. E.g. *Debates, resolutions and other proceedings of the convention of the commonwealth of Massachusetts convened 1788, to ratify the Constitution* (Boston, 1788).

L.C. classes (JK161) under U.S. constitutional history of the federal government.

(b) Conventions convened to form a state constitution: Class under the state. E.g. *Journal of the convention for*

framing a constitution for Massachusetts Bay, 1779–1780.
(Boston, 1832). Class under Massachusetts constitutional
history.

L.C. classes (JK3125–   ) under constitutional history of Massachusetts.

132 Constitutional law of a special subject (e.g. peerage, parliament)

Class with subject.

133 Constitutional powers of an institution (e.g. a court)

Class with other works on that institution and its history,
not under constitutional law. In other words, the history
of an institution and the powers conferred upon it belong together. E.g. *The Supreme court and the Constitution.* By
Charles A. Beard (New York, 1912). Class under Supreme
court, not under constitutional history of the United States
in general.

134 Constitutions, State and national

A work on the constitution of a state of the Union accompanied by the Constitution of the United States: Class
under the state constitution. E.g. *The constitutions of the
United States and of the state of Ohio, 1913;* thoroughly
annotated and indexed by Wm. Herbert Page (Cincinnati,
1913). Class under Ohio, as the purpose of including the
Constitution of the United States is obviously to supplement that of Ohio.

135 State action concerning policy

A work treating of the action of a state or organized body
upon a proposed constitution or political course of action:
Class under the topic acted upon. E.g. *Pennsylvania and
the federal constitution, 1787–1788.* Ed. by John Bach Mc-
Master and Frederick D. Stone (Hist. Soc. of Pa., 1888).
Class under constitutional history of the United States, not
history of Pennsylvania. Cf. Constitutional conventions,
State: 131.

136 Court rolls

Court rolls and similar material, especially when of genealogical or of antiquarian interest, and confined to the affairs of a limited region: Class in local history (not in courts). E.g. *The court rolls of Clitheroe* [England] (Manchester, 1897–1913. 3v.). Class in history of Clitheroe.

ADMINISTRATION

137 Public ownership

(a) Works on municipal ownership: Class in state and industry. E.g. (1) *Municipal ownership in the United States.* By Evans Clark (New York, 1916). (2) *The dangers of municipal ownership.* By Morris E. Jacobs (Omaha, 1933). (3) *Selected articles on municipal ownership.* Ed. by J. E. Morgan (White Plains, N.Y., 1914).

L.C. classes theory of municipal industries (HD4421–) under economic history; D.C. classes municipal ownership (380.167624) under commerce.

(b) Works on public ownership or control of certain utilities: Class by the utility, e.g. telegraph, electric power, not with general works on public ownership or control.— (Los Angeles). E.g. (1) *Government control and operation of telegraph, telephone and marine cable systems, August 1, 1918 to July 31, 1919; acts of Congress . . .* (Washington, 1921). (2) *Municipal electric light managers, their selection, training, salaries and tenure.* By Edna C. Macmahon (Chicago, 1934). (3) *Selected articles on government of telegraph and telephone.* Comp. by K. B. Judson (White Plains, N.Y., 1914).

138 Public works

(a) Works dealing with the administration of public works: Class in administration. E.g. *Municipal public works, their inception, construction, and management.* By S. Whinery (New York, 1903).

(b) Engineering plans and specifications, and regulations, relating to public works: Class in engineering. E.g.

(1) *Planning and control of public works.* By Committee on Recent Economic Changes (Washington, 1930). (2) *Specifications and standards of public works engineering.* By E. E. Russell Tratman (New York, 1933). (3) *Public works inspection.* By William Goldsmith (New York, 1914). (4) *Specifications, schedules, and drawings, Hoover dam power plant.* By U.S. Bureau of Reclamation (Washington, 1930).

139 City planning

Works on city planning: Class in local administration.

Los Angeles does so. Queens Borough writes: "711 is not used. Works on this subject are classed in 352.9, which is divided geographically; 352.973 is not subdivided further."—(Radtke). D.C. classes general works in art (711), but planning of special cities in description (914–919).

Cf. Economic planning: 118.

140 Slum clearance, housing

Works on the problems connected with slums and their elimination: Class in housing. E.g. (1) *A tentative five year plan for slum clearance and low-cost housing in New Jersey.* By the State Housing Authority of New Jersey (Newark, 1934). (2) *Slum reclamation and rehousing.* By the Alley Dwelling Authority for the District of Columbia (Washington, 1936).

Syracuse U. writes: "We have under consideration at present the question of classing slum clearance and housing as 'urbanism' with city planning, rather than with laboring classes (331.8), or with dwellings (728) in an architectural collection."—(Calkins). Plans and specifications for model houses for the poor are of direct value for the architect and, like studies of the hygienic aspects of slums, may require separation from the general subject of slum clearance. D.C. classes esthetic problems of slum clearance in landscape gardening (711), economic and practical problems of housing in economics (331.833).—(D.C. editors).

141 Municipal documents

(a) Documents not distinctly limited to specific subjects: Class in municipal administration.

(b) Documents covering specifically definite subjects:
Class by topic. E.g. Street railway transportation.

The John Crerar Library rule excepts for specific treatment only
publications of public libraries, school boards and jails. "Shelve geographically under local government except publications of public
libraries, of school boards and of city and county jails. Eg. Report
of Chicago Water Commissioners; Report of Chicago Board of Education. Separate documents (not serials) are classed under subject,
e.g. Report of the special Traffic Commission published in 1919."

142 Roman municipalities

Works on the government of the city in the Roman Empire (including Greece): Class under government, not
under municipal government. E.g. *The municipalities of
the Roman empire*. By James S. Reid (Cambridge, 1913).
Class in Roman administration.

The reason for this is that there is practically no line to be drawn
between the government of city and state in antiquity.

L.C. classes in antiquities of Rome (DG87).

143 National economic emergency measures

The above is the title given by the John Crerar Library to a large
collection of material on the "New Deal" and other measures of the
federal government undertaken since 1933. The various "administrations" of these measures are popularly referred to by the initials of
their names, e.g. AAA, CCC, NRA, PWA. An elaborate scheme of
classification, designed to keep all of this material together, has been
drawn up by Miss Harriet E. Penfield, classifier of that library.
There is diversity of procedure among libraries as to the treatment
of these publications.

(a) Works on the national economic emergency measures as a whole: Class under the federal administration.

(b) Works on any one of these measures—organization,
operation, or history: Class by the field of operation. E.g.
(1) *Code of fair competition for the motor bus industry.*
By the NRA (Washington, 1934). (2) *Report of residence
schools and educational camps for unemployed women.* By
the FERA (Washington, 1936). (3) *Labor provisions
for the wholesale food and grocery trade.* By the NRA
(Washington, 1933). (4) *The blue book.* Ed. by the
HOLC (Washington, 1936). (5) *Statistical summary of*

emergency relief activities. By the FERA (Washington, 1937). (6) *The Civilian Conservation Corps program.* By Nelson C. Brown [Washington, 1934]. (7) *War Department regulations; relief of unemployment.* [By the CCC. Washington, 1933].

Examples cited are classed: (1) by L.C. in *motor buses* (HD3616.U452) under economics; by D.C. in land transportation (388.30973). (2) by L.C. in *unemployed women* (HD6093); by D.C. in *public aid* (361.60973). (3) by L.C. in *grocery trade* (HD9321.6); by D.C. in *agricultural products* (338.1), both under economics. (4) by L.C. in *credit* (HG3729.U5); so also by D.C. (332.3130973). (5) by L.C. in *charities* (HV85); by D.C. in *public aid* (361.6). (6) and (7) by L.C. in *forestry* (SD143); so also by D.C. (634.90973).

The D.C. editors write of these measures: "We treat as economic movements identified with the branches of industry concerned and class them respectively under the industry." John Crerar Library, Franklin and Marshall C., and Temple U. keep all publications of this group together under administration, bringing out the field of operation through the subject catalog. The following libraries, in reply to inquiry, class these measures as economic movements identified with the branches of industry concerned: Boston, California U., Cincinnati, Columbia U., Harvard U., Indianapolis, Iowa State C., Library of Congress, Newberry, Princton U., Queens Borough, Minnesota U., Wesleyan U.

144 Federal administration vs. Constitutional history

(a) Works dealing with the functions, operations, services and accomplishments of the federal government: Class in administration.—(Queens Borough).

(b) Works treating of the historical facts, or of the political theories that led to the formation of the Constitution or which have led to its amendment: Class in constitutional history.—(Queens Borough).

L.C. groups together constitutional history and administration (JF–JQ); D.C. separates constitutional law and history (342) and administration (350).

MILITARY SCIENCE

145 Military science

"Distinguish between the conduct of war as an event in national or international history, and the army and navy as strictly military organizations. For example, the history of the German military organization is a special phase of German national life and as such is excluded from the class History. The events in the conduct of a war are, on the other hand, part of the general political history of that country."—(Pettee).

146 Department of a branch of military or naval service

Rules, regulations and registers of a department (e.g. paymaster's) of a branch of military or naval service (e.g. Marine corps) : Class with the branch, not with the corresponding department of the army or navy in general. E.g. *Manual of the paymaster's department of the U.S. Marine corps* (Washington, 1912). Class under Marine corps, not with navy accounting in general.

Example cited is classed by L.C. in naval maintenance (VC53).

147 Army history

(a) History of an army or of a regiment of volunteers during a single war: Class under the war. E.g. (1) *Wellington's army, 1809–1814.* By C. W. C. Oman (London, 1912). Class under Peninsular war. (2) *History of the 9th regiment, New York volunteer cavalry, war of 1861 to 1865.* By Newel Cheney (Jamestown, 1901). Class in regimental histories of the Civil war. Cf. 148e, note.

Examples cited are classed: (1) by L.C. in *Peninsular war* (DC231) under history of France. (2) by L.C. in *regimental histories* (E523.6) under U.S. Civil war.

(b) Histories of militia regiments covering their entire history, or regiments of the regular army: Class under military organization or history. E.g. (1) *History of the Seventh regiment of New York, 1806–1889.* By Emmons Clark (New York, 1890. 2v.). Class in military history of New York. (2) *Cromwell's army, the English soldier during the civil wars, the commonwealth and the protectorate.* By C. H. Firth (London, 1912). Class under history of the British army.

This separation is necessary because the regimental histories of a war cannot be spared from history, while it is out of the question to class all regimental histories there.

Examples cited are classed: (1) by L.C. in state militia of New York (UA364). (2) by L.C. in organization of the British army (UA649).

148 Wars

(a) A war of invasion: Class under the history of the country invaded. E.g. Franco-Prussian war under France.

The wars of the United States may be excepted; yet the tendency to group everything in United States history will be less general now that distant lands like Hawaii, the Philippines, and islands of the West Indies have come into our possession.

(b) In case both countries have been invaded: Class under the country where most of the fighting has occurred.

(c) A revolt of a colony: Class under the history of that colony, not under the history of the mother country. E.g. (1) The Boer war. Class under Transvaal. (2) Harper's *Pictorial history of the war in the Philippines.* Class under Philippine Islands.

The point of this is that if the revolt is suppressed, the account remains local history, and if independence is secured, the classification falls under the number for the new nation.

(d) A war between two countries regarding a colony or dependency of one of these countries: Class under the colony. E.g. *The history of the Italian-Turkish war, September 29, 1911 to October 18, 1912.* By Commodore W. H. Beehler (Annapolis, 1913). Class under history of Tripoli, for control of which Italy and Turkey were fighting.

(e) History of the part taken by a state, county, city or town in a war (e.g. Revolution, Civil war, European war): Class under the history of the state, county, city or town unless the system makes provision for local participation in wars.

This rule does not apply to regimental histories, either collective or individual, which are histories of units forming part of the national armies. Cf. Army history: 147.

L.C. classes history of the participation taken by a state in a war, e.g. U.S. Civil war (E495–), under the war, but that of a county, city or town in local history. D.C. classes state and local participation, e.g. Civil war (973.744–), under the war with local history as an alternative for local participation.

149 Battles and sieges

Class under the war in which they occur, not under local history. E.g. The siege of Paris in the Franco-Prussian war; defense of Verdun in the European war.

The reason is that the actors in such events are part of the armies conducting the war, the battle or siege is an event in the conduct of the war, and while it is also an event in the history of the place, this event must be left to the catalog to bring out.

150 Battlefield memorials, monuments, and commissions

(a) Works on the memorials of a war: Class as topic under the war.

(b) Battlefield memorials, monuments or commissions relating to a particular battle in a war: Class under the battle. E.g. Indiana Antietam Monument Commission.

L.C. classes state memorials or monuments as a topic under the war; but a monument on a particular battlefield under the battle, e.g. Antietam (E474.65). D.C. classes memorials of a particular battle, e.g. Bunker Hill monument, with other monuments of the given war.

151 Classes of persons in a war

The part taken by members of a special class, church or sect in a single war: Classify under the war; preferably in a special subdivision for the class subdivision. E.g. *Catholics and the American revolution*. By Martin M. J. Griffin (Philadelphia, 1907–11. 3v.). Class under Revolution.— (N.Y. State Library; University of California).

The alternative of classing such works under the history of the class, church or sect has this disadvantage, that suitable subdivisions will not ordinarily be practicable.

Diplomatic history of wars. See Diplomatic history of wars: 111.

152 Invasions

Invasion of certain states or territories during the operations of a war: Class under that war, not under the history of the state. Cf. Battles and sieges: 149. E.g. *The British invasion of Maryland, 1812–1815*. By William M. Marine (Baltimore, 1913). Class under War of 1812.

153 Military collective local biography (single war)

Biographical sketches of soldiers from a certain state or town taking part in a single war: Class under the war, preferably in a subdivision for local participation. E.g. (1) *The heroes of Albany, a memorial of the patriot-martyrs of Albany, 1861–1865.* By Rufus W. Clark (Albany, 1867). (2) *Biographical sketches of Illinois officers engaged in the war against the rebellion of 1861.* By James Grant Wilson (Chicago, 1861). Class both under Civil war.

This is also the New York State Library rule. Cf. subsection (e) of Wars: 148e, note.

154 Tactics

Tactics for a special arm of the service, e.g. infantry: Class under that arm, not with general tactics.

155 Engineer corps

(a) Tactics, strategy, drill and general regulations of the technical services of the army, e.g. the engineer corps: Class under military science.—(John Crerar Library).

(b) Works relating to the construction by the engineer corps of military works or to engineering operations: Class under military engineering.—(John Crerar Library).

L.C. classes in *military engineering* (UG) under military science; D.C. in *military engineering* (623) under engineering.

NAVAL SCIENCE

156 Navy

(a) History of the development of the navy of a country: Class in naval organization.

(b) History of naval actions occurring in the history of a country: Class in naval history of the country. E.g. (1) *The naval history of Great Britain.* By William James. (New ed.; London, 1847. 6v.). (2) *The major operations of the navies in the war of American independence.* By A. T. Mahan (Boston, 1913).

The New York State Library classes in *history* of the country. D.C. does likewise. L.C. groups naval history under history of the country, but classes naval operations of a single war under the war, e.g. example cited (2) in American revolution (E271).

157 Marines

(a) History of the organization of the marine corps in a country: Class in naval science.

L.C. has section *marines* (VE) under naval science, and also a topical heading *special troops* under foreign armies, e.g. for Royal marines (UA659.R9). D.C. classes marine corps under naval science (359).

(b) History of the operations, naval or military, of marines: Class in naval history of the country, or as a topic under the wars in which they were engaged. E.g. *The historical records of the Royal marines.* By Lourenço Edye (London, 1893. v.1). Class in naval history of Great Britain.

L.C. separates the naval from the military operations of marines in the World war, classing land operations of the U.S. Marines in D570.348 and naval operations in D570.45; D.C. does the same, in 940.412-.413 for military and 940.45 for naval operations of marines in the war. Use naval history for works covering both fields.

Example cited is classed by L.C. under marines (VE57).

WELFARE

158 Institutions

Hospitals, asylums and other similar institutions: Class geographically, not by type of institution.—(John Crerar Library). E.g. Hospitals for the insane in Illinois. Class in sociology, not in medicine.

159 Hospital reports

Hospital reports and similar material about hospitals, which contain both administrative and clinical material: Class under medicine.—(John Crerar Library).

160 Insurance

Insurance, long a private business based upon the payment, by the insured, of premiums, or upon assessments levied on the funds of fraternal organizations, has broadened into a form of social security, conducted by state agencies, or under federal laws. Even national insurance against war is discussed.

(a) Works on insurance as security based upon the payment of premiums or the like by the insured: Class in insurance. E.g. (1) *Insurance, a practical guide*. By S. B. Ackerman (New York, 1928). (2) *Buying insurance, a problem of business management*. By P. D. Betterley (New York, 1936). (3) *State insurance in the United States*. By David McCahan (Philadelphia, 1929).

(b) Works on insurance supported by the state through direct or indirect taxation: Class in social insurance. E.g. (1) *Social security*. By Edward H. Ochsner (Chicago, 1936). (2) *The quest for security*. By I. M. Rubinow (New York, 1934).

L.C. classes social insurance as *workingmen's insurance*, (HD7090–) under labor, with alternative (HG9500) under insurance; and *state insurance* (HG8925–) under life insurance. D.C. classes *social insurance* (368.4) under insurance, also *workmen's insurance* (331.2544) under labor.

(c) Works on insurance against unemployment or disability, maintained by labor unions: Class under labor. E.g. *Company sickness benefit plans for wage earners*. By Eleanor Davis (Princeton, 1936).

(d) Insurance on other kinds of risks, e.g. automobiles, agricultural stock and crops, timber: Class as topic under the subject.

L.C. classes in casualty insurance (HG9956–); D. C. by topic.

EDUCATION

161 Definition and scope of the class

Education as the "act or process of training by a prescribed or customary course of study or discipline" *(Webster)* is used as a term in classification to cover largely formal training of the mind, not culture by means of libraries or by private reading. Just as "psychology of" a given subject may better be classed with the topic studied, so "study of" a given subject may be concerned more with the methods of approach than with the mental processes involved. A psychological library will class all psychological inquiries under psychology; an educational library will class all "study" of various subjects under teaching of that subject. Other libraries will prefer the subject studied to the process, unless the intent of the author is obviously pedagogic.

162 Vocational guidance

(a) Works on vocational guidance that emphasize the counselor's part and are not related to a single vocation: Class in educational methods. E.g. *Common problems in group guidance, a manual for counselors in secondary schools.* By Richard Day Allen (New York, 1934).

L.C. classes as topic (HF5381) under business; D.C. as topic (371.425) under educational systems.

(b) Works on vocational guidance relating to a particular vocation: Class under the vocation as study and teaching of the subject.—(Queens Borough).

(c) Works on vocations for women: Class in women's work. E.g. *Fifty little businesses for women.* By Mary Raymond Dodge (New York, 1928).

163 Study and teaching of individual subjects

The systems make provision for the study and teaching of the larger subjects, e.g. commerce, science, at the beginning of each division; also under curriculum the teaching of a special branch may be brought out either as a topic or as an alternative to the form heading under subject. Where the system does not provide for specific topics of study or teaching, decision may be made on the basis of the class of persons for whom the book is intended.

(a) Works on the study and teaching of special subjects, written for teachers or formulating a scheme for the curriculum: Class in education.

(b) Works written for students of a subject, or to formulate methods of study or research in the subject: Class under the subject. E.g. *Introduction aux études historiques.*

Par Langlois et Seignobos (Paris, 1905). Class under methodology of history.

164 Normal colleges, empowered to confer degrees

Class with normal schools, not with general colleges.— (John Crerar Library).

165 Colleges

Colleges for the higher education of women, empowered to grant degrees: Class with other colleges or in education of women, according to system. E.g. *Bryn Mawr college, fiftieth anniversary* (Bryn Mawr, 1935).

Classed by L.C. in higher education of women (LD7067.7), so also by D.C. (376.8).

Dewey "provides for classing works about such institutions under higher education of women, with geographic division."—(D.C. editors). John Crerar Library classes all colleges for women along with other degree-conferring colleges.

166 Religious education

(a) Works discussing the introduction of religious teaching into schools or colleges, or the relation of religion to education: Class in education. E.g. (1) *Religious teaching in the public schools.* By Lamar T. Beman (New York, 1927). (2) *Public school religion.* Ed. by Arnold Lunn (London, 1933).

(b) Works on the teaching of religion, whether as catechetics or as training for the ministry or priesthood: Class in religion. E.g. (1) *Religious education as character training.* By Leonid V. Tulpa (New York, 1935). (2) *The religious teaching of the Old Testament.* By Albert C. Knudson (New York, 1918).

L.C. classes religious education (BV1460–), including Sunday schools (BV1500–) under practical theology; education controlled by churches (LC321–) under education. D.C. classes religious education (377) under education, including parochial schools (377.5); Sunday schools (268) under church institutions. L.C. classes education of the clergy (BV4019–) under pastoral theology; D.C. classes as study of religion (207).

167 Dissertations, Doctoral

(a) Bibliography of dissertations on various subjects issued from an individual college or university: Class in bibliography of the college or university.—(Queens Borough).

(b) Bibliography of dissertations on various subjects issued by colleges or universities: Class with general subject bibliographies.—(Queens Borough).

(c) Bibliography of dissertations on a particular subject: Class in bibliography of the subject.

(d) Treat the dissertations themselves like pamphlets. Cf. Pamphlets: 24.

168 Education, State

Reports and other serial publications of American state departments of public instruction: Class under public schools.—(John Crerar Library).

This rule is an alternative to classing strictly by the scope of the reports. State departments, having supervision over state universities and state technical schools, as well as secondary education, cover a wider field than public schools; but the bulk of the material is concerned with elementary and secondary education.

CUSTOMS

169 Duels

Class under biography of the person *challenged*. E.g. Duel of Burr and Hamilton. Class under Hamilton.

The New York State Library rule is the same "unless the other party is the more important person." D.C. does likewise.

170 Pageants

Class together, not under the particular occasion, letting the catalog bring out the events, periods, costumes or other topics represented. Cf. Drama dealing with a special topic: 279a.

Queens Borough writes: "Owing to departmentalization we divide our material on pageants. If the text of the pageant is emphasized, we class in literature; if the emphasis is on the production, we class in 791.6," i.e. public fêtes.

171 Romances, Medieval

Medieval romances dealing with characters that figure in several literatures, e.g. King Arthur: Class by language. E.g. *The vulgate version of the Arthurian romances* (French). Ed. by H. Oskar Sommer (Washington, 1908–16). Class in French medieval romances. The English and the Celtic romances dealing with King Arthur would be classed in English and Celtic romances respectively.

This seems to be the only practicable way of handling this type of literature, although it of course separates material dealing with the same subject. If consistency be deemed by the classifier less important than convenience, all of the literature dealing with the same traditional or mythical character may be grouped together under the character, but there will be some difficulties.

SCIENCE

172 Definition and scope of the class

"The unity of this group lies in its method. Science divides the universe into certain distinct forms of phenomena, physical and mental, and by scientific investigation attempts to learn how these phenomena act. In this class is included only material connected with the scientific study of the various subjects."—(Pettee).

Many new concepts have in recent years been introduced into scientific knowledge, e.g. electrons, protons, wave mechanics, quantum theory, quantum statistics. The system may make provision for these new topics, or a more conservative policy may be observed pending developments. In either case the classifier will do well to keep the newer books separate from the older. This may be effected by introducing a time division when the insertion of a new heading is not deemed advisable.

The practice of the Library of Congress, as stated by C. W. Perley, is: "Recent trends in science and philosophy have affected all recent works more or less. For instance, relativity and quanta. In general they have been assigned definite classification; relativity QC6, quantum theory QC174–QC174.5; but special applications have been classed with the special subject as, gravitation, chemical reactions,

etc., with added entries for the general theory." L.C. examples of
special topics are given below. "D.C. would provide for each new
concept or topic in science under the most closely related subject now
in the table."—(D.C. editors).

173 Application of one science to another

A work on one science or the methods of one science as
applied or adapted to another: Class under the science or
art to which these methods are applied. E.g. *Pedagogical
anthropology*. By Maria Montessori; tr. by Frederic Taber
Cooper (London, 1913). Class in education, because it
treats of the application of the science of anthropology to
education, not *vice versa*.

Example cited is classed by L.C. in *anthropological studies*
(LB1125) under education.

174 Science vs. Engineering

Works on scientific theory as applied in engineering:
Class in engineering. E.g. (1) *Thermodynamics applied to
heat machines*. By E. H. Lewitt (2d ed.; London, 1937).
(2) *Elements of engineering thermodynamics*. By James
A. Moyer . . . (New York, 1935). (3) *Theory of thermi-
onic vacuum tubes; fundamentals, amplifiers, detectors*. By
E. Leon Chaffee (New York, 1933). (4) *Radio receiving
and television tubes including applications*. By James A.
Moyer and John F. Wostrell (3d ed.; New York, 1936).
(5) *Electron tubes and their application*. By John H. More-
croft (London, 1936).

Examples cited are classed: (1) and (2) by L.C. in *thermodynamics* (TJ265) under mechanical engineering; (3) by L.C. in
vacuum-tubes (TK5865) under wireless telegraphy; (4) by L.C. in
vacuum-tubes (TK6565.V3) under wireless telephony; (5) by L.C.
in *vacuum-tubes* (QC544.V3) under physics. D.C. classes (1) and
(2) in *thermodynamics* (621.101) under mechanical engineering;
(3), (4) and (5) in *vacuum-tubes* (621.384132) under electric engineering.

175 Science treated locally

Specific subjects under the physical and biological
sciences, treated locally: Class under the specific subject.

E.g. Volcanoes in Italy. Class under volcanoes, not with physical geology of Italy.

Class under specific subject in paleontology, botany and zoology, instead of by pla'ce. E.g. Cryptogams of North America go under cryptogams, not under flora of North America.

176 Scientific expeditions

(a) Reports of scientific expeditions covering physical and astronomical as well as geographical and biological phenomena: Class in general science.

(b) Reports confined largely to geographical, meteorological, botanical and zoological science: Class in natural history.—(John Crerar Library).

The general library will usually class both types in general science collections.

D.C. classes natural history expeditions with general scientific explorations (508.3) or by country.

(c) Scientific expeditions undertaken to study or record certain groups of phenomena: Class by the subject of the phenomena. E.g. Ocean life.

(d) Narratives of a popular character. Class in travel, irrespective of the topic illustrated, except in scientific libraries. E.g. *The pulse of Asia; a journey in Central Asia illustrating the geographic basis of history.* By Ellsworth Huntington (Boston, 1907). Class in travel or in anthropogeography, according to needs of library.

177 Mathematics

(a) Analytical methods in mathematical procedure, when connected with physical problems: Class under mathematics.—(John Crerar Library). E.g. Treatise on Bessel functions and their applications to physics.

(b) Mathematical works dealing with analytic mechanics: Class under physics.—(John Crerar Library). E.g. (1) Analytic mechanics comprising the kinetics and statics of solids and fluids. (2) Mechanics via the calculus.

L.C. classes the mathematical only (QA802–) under mathematics; D.C. classes mechanics (531) under physics.

(c) General mathematical physics: See Physics: 181b.

(d) Mathematical handbooks for the use of engineers, electricians, physicians, surveyors and other experts: Class with other manuals containing useful tables, statistics and calculators for such users.

There is a decided difference of opinion regarding this rule. The New York State Library says "Depends on the individual book and library." The John Crerar Library rule is: "Handbooks of mathematics for engineers, doctors, housekeepers, etc., class under the application—engineering, medicine, etc."

Such works are in purpose technical, not mathematical, manuals and may consistently be classed with the manuals for technical or professional users. They are too specialized in content to be of use under mathematics.

Cf. Theoretical-applied science: 197.

178 Mathematical theory of statistics

Works on the mathematical theory and technique of statistics, if not given a special bracket under statistics: Class in mathematics.—(Iowa State C.). L.C. divides according as the work is pure mathematical theory or the general theory of statistics. E.g. (1) *Mathematical expectation of product moments of samples drawn from a set of infinite populations.* By Hyman Morris Feldman (St. Louis, 1935). (2) *The statistics of sampling.* By C. H. Richardson (Ann Arbor, Mich., 1936). (3) *Statistics for professional students.* By R. L. A. Holmes (London, 1936).

Examples cited are classed: (1) and (2) by L.C. in *sampling* (probabilities) (QA276.5) under mathematics; by D.C. (519.6), in errors of observation (probabilities). (3) by L.C. (HA29) and D.C. (311) in theory of statistics.

179 Relativity (in science)

Works on relativity in science as a theory or concept: Class in theory of physics rather than in mathematics.—(Wesleyan U.). E.g. (1) *Relativity, the special and general theory.* By Albert Einstein; tr. by Robert W. Lawson (New York, 1931). (2) *Einstein's theory of relativity.* By Max

Born; tr. by Henry L. Brose (London, 1924). (3) *Relativity and reality*. By G. H. Paelian. (2d ed.; New York, 1936). (4) *Beyond Einstein*. By Theodore Stalzer (Philadelphia, 1936).

Wesleyan U. writes: "Books on 'relativity' we formerly classed in mathematics. We have a rather large collection of books in this field and we recently developed a special number under physics [LHR in the Cutter system] to bring this and allied material together." L.C. and D.C. class in physics.

180 Clocks and other instruments for measuring time

(a) Scientific treatises upon the theory of measuring time, adjustment to sun time, etc.: Class under astronomy.

L.C. classes in geodetic astronomy (QB209–); D.C. in *chronology* (529.78) under astronomy.

(b) Descriptive works upon the technical process of manufacturing the works or on both works and decorative cases: Class under manufactures.

L.C. classes in metal manufactures (TS540–); D.C. in mechanic trades (681.113).

(c) Descriptive works confined to decorative cases: Class in art.

L.C. classes in *wooden clock-cases* (NK2720) or in *metal work* (NK7480–) under art; D.C. in *artistic furniture* (749) under art.

181 Physics

(a) Analytical methods in mathematical procedure, when connected with physical problems. See 177a.

(b) General mathematical physics: Class under physics. —(John Crerar Library).

L.C. classes as topic (QC20) under physics; D.C. classes in philosophy of physics (530.151).

182 Atomic physics

"The old distinction that the molecule is the unit for the physicist and the atom for the chemist scarcely holds today. Yet there are works on the atom that look toward physics and others that look toward chemistry."—(Penfield). Separation, especially of the older books from the newer, is desirable.

(a) Works on the atom and its constituents, treating the subject from the physical point of view: Class under physics. E.g. *An outline of atomic physics.* By members of the physics staff of the University of Pittsburgh (New York, 1937).

For varying practice see comment under (b) below.

(b) Works on the atom as a unit of proportion entering into compounds: Class under chemistry. E.g. (1) *Electronic evolution of the atom.* By I. L. Garrison (Phoenix, Ariz., 1928). (2) *Modern views of atomic structure.* By Karl Rast; tr. by W. O. Kermack (London, 1935).

The John Crerar Library writes that as the Dewey classification, 13th ed., used by the library, did not modify 539 to include atomic physics, as the Brussels scheme did, the John Crerar continued to class everything on atoms and subatoms in 541.2, whether the material looked toward physics or toward chemistry. Atomic physics should now go into physics, but the library's collections are too extensive to change at present. The University of Illinois Library has, through Mr. Trotier in consultation with the professor of physics, worked out an expansion of 539.—(Penfield). "D.C. classes most of this material with physical chemistry in 541.2; however, 539.1 is recommended for strictly physical discussions."—D.C. editors). L.C. classes in *molecular and atomic physics* (QC173–).

183 Quantum theory

Works on the quantum theory of the atom: Class in physics. E.g. (1) *The quantum theory of the atom.* By George Birtwistle (Cambridge, Eng., 1926). (2) *Term structure of the non-collinear triatomic molecule of type* X_2Y. By Alexander V. Bushkovitch (Philadelphia, 1934).

Examples cited are classed: (1) by L.C. in *quantum theory* (QC174) under physics; by D.C. in theory of physics (530.1). (2) by L.C. in *triatomic molecule* (QC174.5) under physics; by D.C. as in (1).

184 Quantum mechanics of chemical reactions

Works on the quantum mechanics of chemical reactions: Class in chemistry. E.g. *The quantum mechanics of chemical reactions involving conjugate double bonds.* By Albert Sherman [Lancaster, Pa., 1933].

Example cited is classed by L.C. in *chemical change* (QD501) ; so also by D.C. (541.39).

185 Photoelectric cells

(a) Works of a theoretical character on photoelectric cells: Class in physics. E.g. *Photoelectric cells, their properties, use, and applications.* By Norman Robert Campbell and Dorothy Ritchie (3d ed. ; London, 1934).

(b) Works of an engineering character on photoelectric cells: Class in electrical engineering.—(John Crerar Library). E.g. (1) *The engineering development of photovoltaic cells.* By Dwight K. Alpern (New York, 1932). (2) *Photoelectric cell applications.* By R. C. Walker and T. M. C. Lance (2d ed. ; London, 1935).

L.C. writes: "Not yet put in engineering." Examples cited are classed: by L.C. in *effects of light, X-rays, etc., on the electric discharge* (QC715) under physics. D.C. editors recommend *primary cells* (621.353) under electric engineering.

186 Electronics and industrial applications of the action of electrons

(a) Works of a theoretical character on electrons: Class in physics. E.g. (1) *Electronics.* By Ralph Gordon Hudson (New York, 1932). (2) *Use of electrons in study of electron activated reactions.* By Lloyd Brewster Thomas [Easton, Pa., 1935].

Examples cited are classed: (1) by L.C. in *radioactivity* (QC721) ; by D.C. in physical chemistry (541.3). (2) by L.C. as in (1) ; by D.C. in *chemic dynamics* (541.39) under chemistry.

(b) Works on the application of the action of electrons to industry: Class in electrical engineering.—(John Crerar Library). E.g. (1) *Fundamentals of engineering electronics.* By William G. Dow (New York, 1937). (2) *Electronics; radio, sound, communications, and industrial applications of electron tubes.* [New York, 1930-   ].

L.C. classes electron tubes and vacuum tubes for radio (TK6565.V3) under electrical engineering; D.C. classes them (621.384132) there also.

187 **Photography and photographs**

Technical and scientific works on photography: Class in fine arts or in technology, according to system.

Queens Borough writes: "In order to have the technical and scientific works on photography in the science group, we have used the number 535.8 for photography, subdividing according to the C.D. [Brussels classification]. Collections of photographs, artistic photographs and portraits are still classed in 770." L.C. classes photography (TR) under technology; D.C. (770) under fine arts. Cf. Portraits: 238.

188 **Blueprints and blueprinting**

(a) Blueprinting as a photographic process: Class in photography.

(b) Blueprints for the use of contractors and builders: Class in building plans and specifications.—(Queens Borough).

189 **Natural history**

Periodicals, society publications and other scientific works of collective content, covering geology, paleontology, biology (or natural history in general), botany, zoology, or any three of these subjects: Class under natural history.—(John Crerar Library).

The general library will probably prefer to class such works under general science.

L.C. classes natural history (QH) as a section of science. D.C. classes (574) under biology with country subdivisions, or classes natural history of countries with scientific travels (508.3). Queens Borough uses scientific travels (508.3) for countries, and classes study of natural history under study of science.

190 **Typical examples selected to illustrate nature's processes**

Class by the topic, not by the species (animal or plant) selected to illustrate the process. E.g. *Plant-animals; a study in symbiosis.* By Frederick Keeble (Cambridge, 1910). Class under symbiosis, not in descriptive zoology under convoluta, which is the species selected as an example.

Example cited is classed by L.C. in convoluta (QL391.T9), not in symbiosis (QH548).

Cf. Zoology: 194c.

191 Ethnology

L.C. classes the description of peoples in anthropogeography (GF); D.C. classes in geography and travel (910). L.C. has also a section of *ethnography* for countries under history (E,F,D). D.C. divides racial groups by language (572.8) and races by country (572.9) under ethnology. L.C. has country divisions under anthropogeography (GF500–) and geographic divisions (except for the Americas and Europe) GN590– under anthropology. The distinction between these several divisions is not obvious; but works on primitive peoples and uncivilized tribes should as a rule be classed under the *science* of anthropology, and those on civilized peoples should be placed under *history* in its broad sense.

(a) Description of a single tribe in many aspects—beliefs, customs, language: Class in systematic or local ethnology, not in geography. E.g. *The Bantu past and present; an ethnographical & historical study.* By S. M. Molema (Edinburgh, 1920). Class in ethnology, not with descriptive works on South Africa.

This is the rule of the John Crerar Library and of the New York State Library.

Example cited is classed by L.C. in *Bantus* (DT764.B2) under ethnology of British South Africa.

(b) Travel in a certain region *including* description of the tribe or tribes inhabiting it: Class in travel, except in scientific libraries. E.g. *Hausaland.* By Charles Henry Robinson (London, 1900). Class under travel in central Sudan, not under Hausa as a tribe.

(c) Description of several tribes belonging to the same ethnical group: Class in systematic ethnology. E.g. *The Melanesians.* By R. H. Codrington (Oxford, 1891).

Example cited is classed by L.C. in *Melanesia* (GN668) under anthropology.

(d) Description of several tribes inhabiting the same region but not so related: Class in local ethnology.

(e) Ethnography of a nation: Class under local ethnology.

192 Evolution

Evolution as a subject for classification has endless ramifications; it may cover plants, animals, man, institutions, arts and sciences, even the universe. The literature on evolution cannot now be kept together by classification save by sacrificing its usefulness in many other directions. The grouping of cards under the heading evolution in the subject catalog should suffice for the guidance of students of the subject collectively.

(a) Works on evolution in general: Class under the heading evolution in either biology or philosophy, according to system. E.g. *Evolution, the root of all isms.* By Dan Gilbert (San Diego, Calif., 1935).

L.C. classes evolution (B818) under philosophy; D.C. does likewise (111.62).

(b) Works on the evolution of plants and animals, or on the evolution of man: Class under the subject or field. E.g. (1) *Evolution and animal life.* By David Starr Jordan . . . (New York, 1907). (2) *Man in the making.* By Thomas Graves (New York, 1936). (3) *The evolution and distribution of flowering plants.* By John Muirhead Macfarlane (Philadelphia, 1933).

L.C. classes biological evolution (QH361–) and descent of man (QH368–) under general biology; evolution of plants (QK980–) under botany. D.C. classes biological evolution (575) and descent of man (575.8) under biology; evolution of plants (581.38) under botany.

(c) Works on the evolution of religion, ethics, the state, art, institutions and the like: Class by topic under the system, institution, or activity so treated.

193 Botany

(a) Geographical distribution of plants characterized by their local environment: Class under the type of environment, not with general flora of the country or region in which they are found.—(John Crerar Library). E.g. Mountain flora of Argentina. Class under mountain flora, not with general flora of Argentina.

L.C. classes marine, tropical, and alpine flora (QK930–) under ecology with country divisions under physiographic regions. D.C. classes marine flora (581.92) with oceanic divisions, and tropical and alpine flora (581.524443–4) under ecology.

Queens Borough classes with the flora of the country or region, and puts wild flowering plants of a given region under botany of the region (581.93–.99).

(b) Works describing a single species of plant: Class in systematic botany without reference to the particular aspect under which the plant is viewed, e.g. its ecology.

Plants, Edible and nonedible. See this heading under Agriculture: 220.

194 Zoology

(a) Works describing a single species of animal or group of animals: Class with the systematic works without reference to the particular aspect under which the animal is viewed. E.g. Habits of beavers. Class under beaver, not under habits of animals in general.

(b) Description of the physiology or anatomy of an organ or of the system (nervous, digestive) of a certain animal: Class under the animal, not under the organ.— (John Crerar Library). E.g. The mammary gland of the kangaroo. Class under kangaroo.

(c) But if the animal is used only as an example of a type on which to experiment: Class under the organ or system.—(John Crerar Library). E.g. Development of the cerebral cortex as shown in the rat. Class under cerebral cortex.

Cf. Typical examples (science): 190.

(d) Works on the comparative anatomy or physiology of a special organ or system (i.e. comparing its structure or function in man and in animals): Class in zoology, not in human anatomy.—(John Crerar Library).

The John Crerar Library rule is: "Physiological and anatomical zoology prevails (1) in all cases of comparative physiology and anatomy and (2) over specific subjects in general."

(e) Geographical distribution of animals characterized by their habitat: Class under the type of environment, not with general fauna of the country or region in which the group is found.—(John Crerar Library). E.g. *Biota of the*

San Bernardino mountains. By J. Grinnell (Berkeley, Calif., 1908). Class under mountain fauna.

L.C. classes *mountain fauna* (QH87) under natural history; D.C. has no special topic for the fauna but classes its analogue *marine flora* (581.92), divisible by oceans, under botany. Queens Borough classes in fauna of the country or region. The alternative of classing the example under zoology of California fails to bring out the significant characteristics of the fauna inhabiting the region.

195 Animal psychology

Location of works on animal psychology is a matter of system.

L.C. classes it (QL785) under zoology and also (BF660–) under psychology. D.C. prefers *animal behavior* (591.5) under zoology but has it also (151.3) under psychology; Cutter and California U. class in psychology.

APPLIED SCIENCE. TECHNOLOGY

196 Applied science

Application of physical theories, as of mechanics, hydraulics, sound, light, heat, electricity: Class in useful arts.

"The theoretical distinction between the applied arts and the pure sciences is easily drawn. The pure sciences are concerned only with the discovery and formulation of scientific laws, while the applied arts, taking the results of the pure sciences, are concerned with the methods of making these results of practical service to man. In the classifications, however, it is often impossible to separate pure science from applied science."—(Pettee).

197 Theoretical-applied science

Theoretical-applied science is scientific information for technological workers in special fields or arts, being scientific data selected to cover only such portion of a given science as bears directly upon the attainment of success in a given field or art.

Class under the application, preferably in a special subhead. E.g. (1) *Directly useful technical series* (London). (2) *Handbuch des Bauingenieurs.* (3) *Bibliothèque scientifique de l'ingénieur et du physicien* (Paris). Special examples are: Metric system for engineers; The application of hyperbolic functions to electrical engineering, or of thermodynamics to steam engineering.

"Of late years there has grown up, in connection with most of the applied sciences, notably mechanical engineering, hydraulic engineering and industrial chemistry, an important class of books which deals with the theoretical treatment of the engineering sciences. We think of these as the theoretical-applied type. These books are wholly different in purpose from the purely experimental and laboratory type of investigation which one classifies without question in the pure sciences."—(Kelley).

198 Bacteria

(a) Works on bacteria as a biological class (Schizomycetes): Class in systematic botany.

(b) Works on medical bacteriology—nature of bacteria, their action and influence on the human body: Class in medicine.—(John Crerar Library).

(c) Works on bacteria in their relation to soil, water, food, and in their pathogenic effects on plants and animals: Class by the matter affected by their presence or action, e.g. under agriculture, engineering, or in plant pathology or animal pathology under science.

L.C. classes bacteriology (QR), including classification of bacteria and their relations, both beneficial and pathogenic, under science with alternative reference to other fields.

199 Sport medicine

The prevention and treatment of injuries received in athletic games has been given the name "sport medicine."

(a) Works on sport medicine in general: Class in hygiene or in sports according to system. E.g. (1) *Sportmedizin und olympische spiele* (Sonderausgabe, Deutsche medizinische wochenschr., 1936), Festschrift der sportärzteschaft (Leipzig). (2) *Safety in athletics, the prevention and treatment of athletic injuries.* By Frank S. Lloyd . . . (Philadelphia, 1936). (3) *Training, conditioning and the care of injuries.* By Walter E. Meanwell . . . (Madison, Wis., 1931).

L.C. classes *sport medicine* (GV344) under physical training for sports; D.C. classes in *protection from accidents* (614.8) or in *hygiene of recreation* (613.7) under medicine.

Cf. Physiology of muscular exercise: 120.

(b) Works on the surgical treatment of injuries received in athletics: Class in surgery.—(John Crerar Library). E.g. (1) *Injuries and sport.* By C. B. Heald (London, 1931). (2) *The control of football injuries.* By M. A. Stevens . . . (New York, 1933).

200 Diseases affecting special organs

Works on a general disease, such as cancer or tuberculosis, as affecting a specific organ: Class under the pathology of the organ or part of the body affected, not with general works on the disease.—(John Crerar Library).

201 Surgery

Surgery of a special region, e.g. abdomen, which may be part of a system, e.g. the digestive system: Class under the special region, not under the system of which it forms a part. —(John Crerar Library).

202 Comparative anatomy of domestic animals

Works on the anatomy of domestic animals or on anatomy for veterinarians: Class in veterinary medicine, not in zoology of vertebrate animals.—(Iowa State C.).

L.C. groups veterinary medicine (SF601–) under animal culture and classes *anatomy* (SF761) under it. D.C. classes *anatomy* of domestic animals (636.0891) and *anatomy of the horse* (636.10891) under zootechny, but diseases of domestic animals in veterinary medicine (619).

"D.C. classes preferably with zootechny (636.0891) under agriculture. but alternatively may be clast with veterinary medicine (619)."—(D.C. editors).

ENGINEERING

203 Mechanics

Distinguish experimental mechanics from applied mechanics.

(a) Experimental mechanics: Class in physics; applied mechanics in engineering; celestial mechanics in astronomy. —(John Crerar Library).

(b) Mathematical works dealing with analytic mechanics: Class under physics.—(John Crerar Library). E.g. Mechanics via the calculus.

L.C. classes mathematical works on analytic mechanics (QA802–) under mathematics.

204 Strength of materials

"Strength of materials deals with the various kinds of stresses and their relation to each other and to allied loads, and with the relations between stresses and strains due to loads. It also deals with the strength of engineering materials under stress and with the effect upon strength of variations of the material. The theory of structures deals with the computation of stresses whereby a knowledge is obtained of the proper design to employ in combining the parts of a structure or of a machine economically and properly."— (Queens Borough, summarizing Swain).

(a) Works on strength of materials when applied to measuring, or to measured stresses and deformations in engineering materials: Class in engineering, subdivision "testing."

(b) Strength of materials when applied to testing stresses and strains in building: Class in building or applied mechanics.

The John Crerar Library rule is: "Class strength of materials (resistance of materials) when applied to measuring and measured stresses and deformations in engineering materials under general engineering, i.e. testing of engineering materials with reference to their fitness in engineering. When strength of materials connotes calculation of stresses and strains in the design of structures, class under theory of structures."

L.C. classes stresses and strains in the construction of bridges and roofs (TG265) under engineering; of buildings (TH845–) under building. D.C. classes stresses and strains in bridges and roofs (624.17) under engineering; in buildings (721) under architectural construction.

205 Machine design and drawings

Works on mechanical drawing in the field of designs for the construction of machines: Class by subject of the drawing under mechanical engineering, not in drawing, under art.—(Queens Borough).

206 Welding

The processes of welding include autogenous, oxyacetylene, thermit, electric arc and others.—(Queens Borough).

Works on any kind of welding: Class together in millwork engineering.—(Queens Borough).

Queens Borough writes: "We have adopted the C.D. [Brussels classification] number for welding and include all methods under the number 621.791. This proves helpful in reference work and saves checking of the subject catalog." This brings welding near forging.

L.C. classes welding as a topic in electric welding (TK4660), metal manufactures (TS227), and mechanic trades (TT211). D.C. classes welding under metal manufactures (671).

207 Tools

No system of classification can well subdivide the class Tools so minutely as to take in every kind of tool used in the arts and manufactures. Moreover, tools are closely connected with the processes in which they are used. Hence it is neither practicable nor desirable to keep all kinds of tools together. Cf. Manufactures: 225.

208 Tools, Hand

Class hand tools with the art in which they are used, preferably in a suitable subdivision; tools used in many different arts or crafts, e.g. knives, saws, may be classed together in an alphabetical arrangement.

"The D.C. now has no special place for hand tools. Probably it would be best to class them in an alphabetical arrangement, e.g. adzes, files, saws, etc., either in a place following machine tools or under the section devoted to mechanic trades. It is best to keep hand tools together."—(Kelley).

"The form division *instruments, apparatus* (078) may be used to separate books on tools from books on the general subject."—(D.C. editors).

209 Tools, Machine

(a) Works on the manipulation of machine tools: Class under mechanical engineering. E.g. Milling machines, perforating machinery.

(b) Works on their manufacture: Class under manufactures.

(c) Machinery for special technical processes: Class with process under manufactures. E.g. Textile machinery with textile manufactures; paper-making machinery with manufacture of paper.

The John Crerar Library rule is: "Class manipulation of machine tools and discussion of different kinds under mechanical engineering. Class manufacture of such tools under manufactures. Class special machinery, as textile machinery, wood-working machinery, under manufactures."

MINING ENGINEERING

210 Geophysical prospecting

Works on geophysical methods of prospecting, especially for oil: Class in economic geology.—(John Crerar Library). E.g. *The principles & practice of geophysical prospecting.* By the Imperial Geophysical Experimental Survey (Cambridge, 1931).

L.C. classes *geophysical prospecting* (TN269) under mineral industries. D.C. classes it in mining engineering (622.1) or according to the point of view.—(D.C. editors).

MILITARY ENGINEERING

211 Artillery

Works on the efficiency of the artillery system as a whole: Class under gunnery.—(John Crerar Library).

212 Map-reading, Military

Class under military topography in military engineering, not under military geography in military science.—(John Crerar Library).

213 Military aeronautics

Class under military engineering, not under aeronautics. —(John Crerar Library).

MECHANICAL ENGINEERING

214 Trailers for automobiles

(a) Works on the building of trailers for automobiles: Class in building of automobiles. E.g. (1) *How to build trailers.* Ed. by Thomas A. Blanchard (Greenwich, Conn., 1937). (2) *Trailer engineering; passenger car trailer design.* [By] Ray F. Kuns (Trotwood, O., 1934).

(b) Works on the use of trailers for touring or in business: Class in touring or as a topic under traveling. E.g. (1) *The trailer for pleasure or business.* By Winfield A. Kimball . . . (New York, 1937). (2) *Touring with tent and trailer.* By Winfield A. Kimball (New York, 1937). (3) *The trailer home, with practical advice on trailer life and travel.* By Blackburn Sims (New York, 1937).

Examples cited are classed: (1) by L.C. in touring by automobile (GV1023); so also by D.C. (796.7). (2) by L.C. in touring by automobile (GV1023); by D.C. in camping (796.54). (3) by L.C. as in (2); by D.C. in *trailers* (629.2262) under automobile engineering.

(c) Works specifically on trailers as habitations to be occupied continuously as such, or on their use as chapels, theaters, traveling libraries, exhibit rooms or salesrooms for merchandise, or for other purposes: Class by use or subject.

The trailer as thus adapted becomes merged with the kind of object that it resembles; or it is used as a means to attain a given end. The difficulty in the case of the trailer used as a dwelling lies in the fact that, being on wheels and subject to traffic regulations, it may be treated as a vehicle; while, as subject to the building code governing size of living rooms and to sanitary regulations, as well as liable to be taxed as a building, it may be classed in housing. When more than one use is considered in a work, prefer 214b.

L.C. makes a special topic for trailers under automobiles (TL297), as also does D.C. (629.2262).

215 Radio

The radio has become an agency in many lines of work. The importance of books showing specific applications of the radio, e.g. to navigation, advertising, education, or music, lies rather in the results attained by the use of the radio than in the radio itself as a means of attaining them. The subject catalog will bring out its various uses.

(a) Works on the construction of the radio and its accessories: Class in *wireless telephony* under engineering. E.g. (1) *Radio construction and repairing.* By James A. Moyer . . . (4th ed.; New York, 1933). (2) *The radio antenna handbook.* Ed. by Frank C. Jones . . . (Los Angeles, 1936).

(b) Works on special uses and applications of the radio: Class by the field of use. E.g. (1) *Safety of life at sea through the use of radio.* By the Committee on Commerce (Washington, 1937). (2) *A decade of radio advertising.* By Herman S. Hettinger (Chicago, 1933). (3) *Present and pending applications to education of radio and allied arts.* By National Advisory Council on Radio in Education (Chicago, 1936). (4) *Men and radio music.* By Peter W. Dykema [New York, 1935?].

Examples cited are classed: (1) by L.C. in nautical *signaling* (VK397); by D.C. in protection of travelers (614.864). (2) by L.C. in *radio broadcasting* (HF6146.R3) under advertising; so D.C. (659.1). (3) by L.C. in *radio in education* (LB1044.5); by D.C. (371.3338) under education. (4) by L.C. in *radio and music* (ML68); by D.C. in value of music (780.13).

(c) Works on the technique of broadcasting: Class as topic in radio engineering.

L.C. classes broadcasting (TK6570.B7) under electrical engineering, D.C. does likewise (621.384193).

(d) Works on the writing of plays for broadcasting by radio, or of "script" to be followed in doing so: Class in special topic under dramatic composition. E.g. (1) *Learn to write for broadcasting.* By Claude Hulbert (London, 1932). (2) *Writing for broadcasting.* By C. Whitaker-Wilson (London, 1935).

The special technique required in writing plays for broadcasting seems to lie in presenting the action adequately to an audience that cannot see it.

L.C. classes in *radio plays* (PN1992) under drama; D.C. with *photoplays* under theater (792).

216 Air conditioning

(a) Works on air conditioning as a mode of ventilating buildings, railroad trains, and other abodes occupied either permanently or transiently: Class in sanitary engineering. —(John Crerar Library). E.g. (1) *Practical air conditioning.* By Harold L. Alt (Chicago, 1936). (2) *The Carrier-safety system for air conditioning railway passenger cars.* (Chicago, 1934).

Alternative is to class with construction of the building or vehicle ventilated. L.C. classes air conditioning of buildings (TH7687) under building; so also does D.C. (697.9). L.C. classes air conditioning of railway cars (TF453) under railroad engineering; D.C. does likewise (625.23).

(b) Works on air conditioning as a mode of preserving food and other perishable things: Class in refrigeration. E.g. *Audels answers on refrigeration, ice making, and air conditioning.* [By Charles E. Booth] (New York, 1937).

Example cited is classed by L.C. in *refrigeration* (TP492) under chemical technology; by D.C. in refrigeration (621.56) under mechanical engineering.

AGRICULTURE

217 Serials, Agricultural

Serial publications (periodicals, annuals, etc.) of agricultural boards and experiment stations: Class under the geographical divisions of agriculture, not with general agricultural serials.—(John Crerar Library).

218 Soil erosion and flood control

Erosion of soil through unwise agricultural treatment, wind storms, floods and other agencies forms the subject of works of much wider scope than those on soils as adapted

for the raising of certain crops or for grazing. Soil erosion
and flood prevention are closely connected, as Indianapolis
Public Library points out, and are parts of the same problem; yet soil is a heading under agriculture and under
geology, while flood prevention comes under engineering.
Tree planting, another aspect of the same problem, comes
under forestry. The classifier can scarcely succeed in doing
justice by classification to the whole subject of soil erosion;
he must leave that end to be attained by the subject catalog.

(a) Works on soils in general or as a natural factor in
agriculture—raising of crops, grazing, or tree-culture:
Class in agriculture or as a topic under geology, according
to system. E.g. (1) *Conservation of the soil.* By A. F.
Gustafson (New York, 1927). (2) *The cost of soil erosion, with control suggestions.* By H. H. Bennett (Springfield, Ill., 1934).

Examples cited are classed: (1) and (2) by L.C. in *soil erosion*
(S623) under agriculture; by D.C. the same (631.45).

(b) Engineering works on flood control, reclamation,
headwaters control: Class in hydraulic engineering. E.g.
(1) *The scientific aspects of flood control.* By F. A. Silcox
. . . (New York, 1936). (2) *Headwaters control and use.*
By Upstream Engineering Conference (Washington, 1937).

219 Marketing of farm produce

(a) Works on the marketing of farm produce by the
farmer or through cooperative groups: Class in farming.—
(Queens Borough).

(b) Works on the marketing of farm produce by middle-
man, wholesaler, or retailer: Class in business.—(Queens
Borough).

220 Plants, Edible and nonedible

(a) Works on the cultivation of edible plants: Class in
agriculture.—(New York State Library).

(b) Works on the cultivation of nonedible plants: Class
in horticulture.—(New York State Library).

INDUSTRIES

221 Business methods

Accounting, advertising, bookkeeping, business manuals for special lines, e.g. industries, trades, institutions: Class under accounting, advertising, or theory of business, subdividing in the order of the classification.—(John Crerar Library). Or subdivide by industries alphabetically.

"This has been one of our most helpful and effective devices for both reference librarian and public alike. We follow such a device in several places. The Library of Congress follows this practice also." —(Kelley). Dewey has not yet subdivided accounting or advertising in that way; but "under business methods 658.92–.999 may be divided by industry like 620–699. Thus hardware business would be 658.971." —(D.C. editors).

Cf. Works for technicians: 38.

222 Chemical industries

Class under chemical technology, not under engineering. —(John Crerar Library).

223 Frozen foods

New literature on frozen foods differs from the older on refrigeration, according to the John Crerar Library, although the Dewey number for foods (664) in chemical technology has been used for it. The Library of Congress reports that no specific number has yet been assigned to frozen foods, but the classification will probably be under cold storage.

Class, pending new developments, under refrigeration. E.g. *The freezing preservation of fruits, fruit juices, and vegetables.* By Donald K. Tressler and Clifford F. Evers (New York, 1936).

Example cited is classed by L.C. in *cold storage* (TP493) under chemical technology; so by D.C. in *preservation of food* (664.8).

224 Metals

(a) History and science of metals: Class under metallography (metallurgy), not in chemistry or geology.—(John Crerar Library).

(b) Tempering, hardening, heat treatment of metals: Class under metal manufactures, not under metallurgy.— (John Crerar Library).

Queens Borough classes tempering, hardening and heat treatment of metals in metallurgy.

225 Manufactures

Advice as to the best treatment of works on manufactures is given by Mr. Dewey in a note under 670 of his classification.

226 Outbuildings and enclosures for animals

(a) Plans for dog kennels, bird houses and the like: Class with works on the care, keeping, and breeding of these animals.

Queens Borough classes all under architecture. The practical end to be served by such structures, and the close connection between the habits and needs of the animal with its housing will be served by following the rule as given.

L.C. classes in animal culture, e.g. dog kennels in SF428; D.C. classes outbuildings in architecture (728.9), and housing of domestic animals in agriculture (636.0831). L.C. provides, however, for dovecotes in architecture (NA8370), and for bird houses (QL676.5) under birds in zoology.

ART. FINE ARTS

227 Definition and scope of the class

"The term art as used by the classifications is restricted to the 'fine arts.' Both the fine arts and the practical arts deal with the methods of putting into concrete form ideas which are practically useful or esthetically pleasing to man, and the line between the two cannot be very sharply drawn. The fine arts cover the material relating to sculpture, the graphic arts, drawing, design, painting, carving, engraving, architecture and the decorative arts."—(Pettee).

228 Animals in art

Class in art, not in zoology.

The works treating of these topics give little information, even at their fullest, about animals as such, but tell how they are viewed and represented as subjects of art, and explain their significance and symbolism.

L.C. classes animals in art as a topic under the several fine arts; D.C. classes painting of animals (758) under art, and symbolical representations (246.5) under ecclesiology.

Distinguish pictures of animals for educational purposes, to be classed under the kind of animal, from the work of artists in which the animals are features of the painting or drawing.

229 Illumination of manuscripts and books

(a) A work on the illuminations or illustrations used in a certain class of books (e.g. missals) : Class under illumination or book illustration, not under the topic treated in the book nor under the bibliography of that class of books. E.g. *Études sur l'art de la gravure sur bois à Venise; les missels imprimés à Venise de 1481 à 1600.* Par le duc de Rivoli (Paris, 1896). Class under wood engraving.

The subject catalog will bring out the topic treated in the book when desirable.

(b) Description of an individual book or manuscript (e.g. the Grimani breviary) : Class next to the book described, whatever the topic.

230 Illustrations

The illustration of books covers the making of the drawing, etching or painting to be reproduced, the technical processes involved in preparing the blocks to be used in printing the illustration, and the actual printing. Queens Borough calls attention to a Dewey number (002) to cover the book, the science of the book, history of the book, and book arts.

(a) Class by the subject of the text, not as the work of the illustrator, unless the text is merely descriptive of the artist's work. E.g. *Rowlandson's Oxford.* By A. H. Gibbs (London, 1911). Treats of Oxford in Rowlandson's day and reproduces Rowlandson's water colors for the first time, but the illustrations are embellishments, not the topic of the book; hence class under Oxford university.

(b) Illustrations taken from the books of an individual

author: Class under book illustration. E.g. *Les illustrations des écrits de Jérome Savonarole publiés en Italie au xv. et xvi. siècle.* Par Gustave Gruyer (Paris, 1879). Class under book illustration. Subject catalog will, of course, make an entry under Savonarola.

The reasons for this are: (1) The intent of the author is to write on book illustration and not on the subjects treated by the author illustrated; (2) the personal interest is subordinated to the art interest; (3) the character of the treatise renders it, as a rule, of no use to the student of the subjects treated by the author illustrated. Example cited is classed by L.C. in wood engraving in Italy (NE1152).

(c) Text accompanied by illustrations of artistic significance, whether by one or more artists: Class by subjects. E.g. *The genus Iris.* By William Rickatson Dykes. With forty-seven coloured drawings (Cambridge, 1913).

An illustrated work on flowers will undoubtedly be useful to the artist, to the book illustrator, and to the youthful reader in search of pictures; but it is intended to represent flowers as they are and should be classed in botany unless professedly written for the artist. Example cited is classed by L.C. by topic (SB413.I8) under flower culture.

(d) Plates exhibiting the work of a single artist, not accompanied by continuous text: Class with biography (and work) of the artist. E.g. *Albrecht Dürers sämtliche kupferstiche* [hrsg.] Von Franz Friedrich Leitschuh (2.aufl.; Berlin, c1912).

Example cited is classed by L.C. in *Dürer* (NE654.D9) under German engraving.

Mechanical drawing. See Machine designs and drawings: 205.

231 Architectural styles

(a) Description of a style of architecture that is characteristic of a certain *period* in a given country: Class under architecture in that country, subdivided by period, not in orders of architecture. E.g. (1) *Architecture of the renaissance in England 1560–1635.* By J. Alfred Gotch (London, 1894. 2v.). Class in English architecture (16th–17th

century). (2) Georgian architecture. Class in 17th-18th
century period.

This rule will apply only to names of periods in a single country,
not to orders, i.e. Ionic, Corinthian, which may be found in any part
of the world and are not, therefore, of national significance.
L.C. classes together architecture of the renaissance *style* with
country subdivisions (NA510–); but Tudor, Elizabethan, Queen
Anne, Georgian, American Colonial, by *period* under the architecture
of special countries (NA701–), with alternative under style. D.C.
divides the modern styles (724) by country.

(b) Works on modern building in styles that derive their
names from periods, e.g. Queen Anne, Colonial: Class
under type of building.

L.C. classes Colonial style of country house in *country homes*
(NA7573). D.C. divides modern styles (724) by country, but not
types of building by style.

232 Buildings, Individual

(a) Class description or history of an individual building, e.g. a library, church, or monastery, in architecture.

(b) Class special details of a single building in general
description of the building, not under the topic. E.g. Sculpture of Strasbourg Cathedral. Class in architecture, not in
sculpture.

The New York State Library classes by topic. L.C. classes sculpture of individual buildings, e.g. the Baptistry of Florence doors, in
sculpture. D.C. does likewise.

(c) History of individual houses: Class in architecture
if all historical data relating to edifices are by system classed
there; otherwise in history or genealogy. E.g. *History of
the Oliver, Vassall and Royall houses in Dorchester, Cambridge and Medford.* By Robert Tracy Jackson (Boston,
1907). A peculiar case; the primary intent of the book is to
give the history of certain houses, i.e. the edifices; but the
families who occupied them were related to one another.
Class in genealogy.

Example cited is classed by L.C. in genealogy of the Oliver family
(CS71.O48).

Cf. Historic houses: 319; Literary shrines: 314.

233 Dedication of buildings

Class under the subject represented by the building; e.g. class dedication of a church under church history, a library under libraries, a historical museum under local history.

234 Gems and precious stones

(a) Works on the engraving of designs on gems and precious stones: Class in engraved gems. E.g. (1) *La gravure en pierres fines, camées et intailles.* Par Ernest Babelon (Paris, 1894). (2) *The handbook of engraved gems.* By C. W. King (London, 1866).

Examples cited are classed: by L.C. in *gems* and *engraved stones* (NK5550, 5525); by D.C. in *gems* (736) under sculpture.

(b) Works on the polishing and mounting of precious stones: Class in jewelry under manufactures.—(Los Angeles). E.g. (1) *Treatise on the art of amateur lapidary.* By Charles L. Shimmel (Madera, Calif., 1936). (2) *Gems, how to know and cut them.* By H. L. Thomson [Los Angeles, 1934].

Examples cited are classed: (1) by L.C. in *precious stones* (TS752) under manufacture of jewelry; by D.C. (679) under manufactures. (2) by L.C. as in (1); by D.C. (549) under mineralogy.

235 Woven fabrics

(a) Works on ornamental woven fabrics, e.g. basketry, rugs, carpets, expressive of the handwork of the weaver or otherwise artistic: Class in ornamental design.—(Los Angeles). E.g. (1) *Decorative textiles.* By George Leland Hunter, with 580 illustration, 27 plates in colour (London, 1918). (2) *Carpet designs & designing.* By Frederick J. Mayers (Benfleet, Eng., 1934).

L.C. classes ornamental textiles, such as costume, rugs, carpets, tapestries, upholstery and wall-hangings, in art applied to industry (NK); D.C. classes them (745) in fine arts.

(b) Works on the technical or commercial manufacture of woven goods: Class in manufactures.—(Los Angeles). E.g. (1) *Basket pioneering.* By Osma Palmer Couch (New York, 1933). (2) *Elementary textile design and fabric structure.* By John Read (New York, 1931). (3) *Mechanical fabrics.* By George B. Haven (New York, 1932). (4) *Textile fibers and their use.* By Katharine Paddock Hess. Ed. by B. R. Andrews (Chicago, 1936).

Examples cited are classed by L.C. in *textile industries* (TS1300–), by D.C. in *textiles* (677) ; both under manufactures.

236 Painting

(a) Works on the painting of some subject (e.g. landscape, flowers, portraits) in oil or in water-color: Class in art under the subject, not under oil or water-color painting. E.g. *The art of landscape painting in oil colour.* By Sir Alfred East (Philadelphia, 1913). Class in landscape painting.

L.C. divides both painting (ND1290–) and water-color painting (ND2190–) by subjects; D.C. divides only painting by subjects (753–758).

(b) Work of artists, whatever may be the prevailing type or subject of their paintings: Class under the school or under the nationality of the artist, according to system.

Queens Borough writes: "Reserve 750 to 758 for discussion of these subjects [epic, genre, ecclesiastical, historical, portrait, landscape]. Works of artists are classed in 759 according to the artist's nationality." L.C. has subhead *special artists,* e.g. sculptors, painters, under the history of the different branches of art in special countries. D.C. subdivides biography of artists under 927, or distributes by subject.

237 Art processes (e.g. etching)

Class under each special process its history, technique, history and illustrative material.

The alternative is to put collections of etchings or works on them under the wider heading Engraving. This is contrary to the principle of close classification and is not recommended. The student of engraving must look under its subdivisions and the student of etching must look under engraving, to find all the resources of the library.

238 Portraits

(a) General collections of portraits, accompanied by biographical sketches: Class in biography, not in art. E.g.

Portraits of illustrious personages of Great Britain (London, 1840. 10v.).

(b) Individual portraits: Class in biography of the individual. E.g. *Life portraits of William Shakespeare.* By J. Hain Friswell (London, 1864).

L.C. classes in painting (N7628,7639) except Shakespeare.

(c) Collections of portrait paintings (reproduced) without text: Class in painting.

(d) Collections of portrait engravings without text: Class in engraving.

(e) Collections of portrait medals (reproduced): Class under medals.

Works confined to medals representing one individual may go with portraits in biography of the person. E.g. *Catalogue des monnaies et des médailles Napoléoniennes.* Par Victor Tourneur (Bruxelles, 1921).

(f) Collections of busts (reproduced): Class in sculpture.

(g) Selective collections portraying a special *class* of persons: Class in biography of that class. E.g. *Portrait medals of Italian artists of the renaissance.* By G. F. Hill (London, 1912). Class under Italian art and artists.

In case of doubt, choose the class of persons in preference to the material of the portrait.

Example cited is classed by L.C. in Italian *medals* (NK6352) under art.

Cf. Photography and photographs: 187.

MUSIC

239 Definition and scope of the class

The term "music," as used in classification, is ambiguous. It may connote scores, or it may cover the whole field of musical literature as well as musical compositions. The term "score," while properly applied to a sheet or series of sheets on which "parts" to be played by *several* musical instruments are represented, is popularly and conveniently used for any piece of music. E.g. the music of Bach's "Gavotte" for violin (alone) is not properly a score; neither is Chopin's "Funeral march" for the piano. But the "scoring" of the two lines for right and left hand in piano music has led to the popular use of "score" to denote any two-hand music or songs with piano accompaniment. Definitions of musical terms used in cataloging music may be found in convenient form in an appendix to L. R. Mc-Colvin's *Music in public libraries.*

240 Music vs. Poetry

(a) Words and tunes only, without accompaniment: Class as music unless the tunes are very subordinate to the purpose of the book.

(b) Words and tunes with accompaniment: Class as music.

241 Music vs. Drama

(a) The complete text of a play accompanied by incidental music:. Class in literature.—(Los Angeles). E.g. (1) *The princess marries the page, a play* [with facsimile of original music composed by Deems Taylor]. By Edna St. Vincent Millay (New York, 1932). (2) *Hellas, a lyrical drama.* By Percy Bysshe Shelley; the choruses set to music by William Christian Selle (London, 1886).

Examples cited are classed: (1) by L.C. and by D.C. in American individual authors. (2) by L.C. and by D.C. in English individual authors.

(b) Lyrics or other selections from a play, accompanied by incidental music: Class in music.—(Los Angeles). E.g. (1) Jean Sibelius' "Valse triste." (Aus der music zu Arvid Jarnefelt's drama *Kuolema).* (2) Sibelius' incidental music to Shakespeare's *Tempest.* (3) "You were there," from *Shadow play.* By Noel Coward (London, 1935).

These lyrics differ musically in no respect from any poem set to music; since songs are usually poems set to music, the interest is in the songs as such.

Examples cited are classed: (1) and (2) by L.C. in incidental dramatic music (M1518); so also by D.C. in dramatic music (782). (3) by Los Angeles in music.

(c) A collection of poems, taken from the works of an individual author, e.g. Shakespeare, and set to music: Class in music. E.g. (1) *Songs from "Alice in Wonderland,"* by Lewis Carroll, music by H. Fraser-Simson (London, 1932). (2) *Kirchenscene aus "Faust."* [Words by Goethe, music by Richard Wagner] (Regensburg, 1933).

The literary associations of the songs may be left to the subject catalog to bring out, although a special collection on an author like Shakespeare may attract musical tributes and settings.

Examples cited are classed: (1) by L.C. in songs (M1997.S59) ; by D.C. in children's songs (784.624). (2) by L.C. in incidental dramatic music (M1518) ; by D.C. in dramatic music (782).

(d) Music composed to accompany the musical rendition of a play, or even as incidental to it: Class in music. E.g. (1) *Ein sommernachtstraum von Shakespeare,* Musik von Felix Mendelssohn Bartholdy (Leipzig). (2) *Peer Gynt von H. Ibsen.* Musik von Edvard Grieg (Leipzig, 1908).

Examples cited are classed: (1) by L.C. in incidental dramatic music (M1513). (2) by L.C. in incidental music (M1510). D.C. editors write: "(b), (c), (d) alternatively may be classed by attraction in literature with the play."

(e) Pageants for which incidental music is merely indicated as, e.g. by titles of favorite or popular songs: Class with other pageants, not under music. Cf. Pageants: 170.

242 Musical criticism

(a) Criticism of the works of a composer: Class with his biography or with his works, according to system.

(b) Criticism of a single composition or group of similar compositions limited to a special class, e.g. sonatas: Class in criticism of that kind of music, not with the biography of the composer. E.g. (1) *Beethoven's pianoforte sonatas explained.* By Ernst von Elterlein [i.e. E. Gottschald] (London, 1898). (2) *Mozart's operas, a critical study.* By Edward J. Dent (London, 1914).

Class (1) under sonatas and (2) under opera. L.C. keeps all works about a composer together, except analytical guides for instruction (MT90-).

Cf. Individual biography of musicians: 335.

243 Dramatic music. Opera

(a) Operatic scores, whether full (i.e. with vocal and orchestral parts shown completely) or vocal (i.e. with vocal and instrumental parts condensed, usually for piano) : Class under operas.

(b) Songs or selections from a single opera: Class with that opera.—(Queens Borough).

(c) Songs selected from several operas: Class with songs.—(Queens Borough).

(d) Overtures that form part of an opera or oratorio: Class with the opera or oratorio.—(Queens Borough). But if detached, class in orchestral music.

(e) Orchestral pieces like an overture in form, e.g. Johannes Brahms' "Tragic overture," illustrating a dramatic or graphic subject: Class in orchestral music.—(Queens Borough).

(f) Scenes from an opera, with either vocal or instrumental score: Class with the opera.—(Queens Borough).

For arrangements for piano see Arrangements of music: 250.

244 Librettos

(a) Works on librettos in general: Class with works on the opera. E.g. (1) *Antenati del libretto d'opera.* [By] Ulderico Rolandi (Roma, 1930). (2) *Dichtung und musik der deutschen opernarien, 1680-1700.* Von Irmtraud Schreiber (Bottrop i.W., 1934).

Examples cited are classed: (1) by L.C. in dramatic music (ML1702.R73) ; by D.C. in works of dramatic authors (781.961) under music. (2) by L.C. in works on German opera (ML1729.2) ; by D.C. in German grand opera (782.3).

(b) Librettos of grand operas, or of operas containing both sung and spoken dialog and lyrics: Class with works on the operas, whether in musical literature or with the music itself, according to system. E.g. (1) *Carmen* [libretto]. By Henri Meilhac and Ludovic Halévy [music by Bizet] (Norman, Okla., 1935). (2) *The barber of Se-*

ville [libretto]. Composed by Rossini (Philadelphia, 1822). (3) *Aïda* [libretto] music by Giuseppe Verdi (New York, 1911).

Examples cited are classed: (1) by L.C. in *librettos* (ML50.B625) under musical literature; by D.C. in French drama (842.89). (2) and (3) by L.C. in *librettos* (ML50); by D.C. in grand operas (782.5).

(c) Plays that have been used for librettos of operas and are printed as plays without the music: Class in drama under the name of the author of the words. E.g. (1) *Carmen, an opera,* the original libretto by H. Meilhac and L. Halévy (London, 1932). (2) *The complete plays of Gilbert and Sullivan* (New York, 1936).

The alternative is to class the "words of the opera" with the opera, whether lines of music are included in the text or not. Such librettos differ but little from those that contain snatches of music; they will undoubtedly be used by those who wish to learn the story of a given opera or to familiarize themselves with the dialog. Yet L.C. and D.C. class librettos issued without the music in drama. An analogy is a play arranged for acting (see 276c), which is classed in drama, not in theater. A musical collection will of course keep all librettos together.

245 Instrumental music

Music written, adapted, or arranged for a given instrument: Class all kinds together under music for that instrument, not separated either by original form of the composition or by kind of composition. E.g. Pianoforte arrangements of operas (without words) or of symphonies: Class with pianoforte music, not with operas or orchestral music. But pianoforte arrangements of operas *with the words* are the same as vocal scores and go with operas.

"All works which will be used by the performer on a given instrument must be together without regard to the nature of the music. Pianoforte scores of operas, piano arrangements of symphonies, concertos, etc., are works for the pianist and must be classified with pianoforte music and not with operatic or orchestral music, as the case may be."—(L. R. McColvin. *Music in public libraries,* p.37-38).

246 Songs

(a) Songs and ballads without music: Class in literature.

(b) Songs and ballads set to music or accompanied by tunes: Class in music.

The only uncertainty arises in classing some collections of old "Songs," i.e. poems, in which occasional tunes are introduced. The intent of the author so far as ascertainable, should determine whether such a book is music or poetry.

(c) Songs of one composer: Class with individual songs, (784.3), not in collections (784.8).—(Queens Borough).

247 Pianoforte music

Dramatic, orchestral, vocal or music of whatever type, arranged for pianoforte alone: Class in pianoforte music. Cf. Arrangements of music: 250.

248 Duets, Instrumental

Class by the solo instrument. E.g. Duets for piano and violin. Class under violin music.

"The rule for all instrumental duets is to classify them as though they were music for the instrument *other than* the piano or organ. Other duets are very rare, but with them the only rule would be to classify the work according to the instrument which has the higher average compass, since that instrument will naturally claim a larger share of the melodic material."—(L. R. McColvin. *Music in public libraries,* p.40).

L.C. classes music for piano with other instruments (M217-) under piano.

249 Chamber music

L. R. McColvin's definition and delimitation of chamber music is a useful one for the classifier to bear in mind: "Chamber music is that music which is written for combinations of three or more players, primarily intended not for public performance, but for rendering in a room (though that is merely a theoretical point) and in which none of the parts is intended to be performed by more than one player. This last is an important element in the definition. If it were intended that parts should (or could) be duplicated the

work would belong to the genre of orchestral music."—
(Music in public libraries, p.39).

250 Arrangements of music

Class under music of the instrument for which the arrangement is made, not by the kind of composition as originally written. E.g. Potpourri of operatic airs for the piano; Beethoven's symphonies, arranged for four-hand rendition. Class under pianoforte music.

"Vocal scores" of operas are condensed scores, not arrangements. Class with the originals. But put choruses, selected or adapted from operas, with choruses, not with the original operas.

THEATER

251 Drama vs. Theater

Distinguish drama in the sense of literature from theater in the sense of acting.

The two terms are frequently used interchangeably by writers, so that the title-page should always be interpreted by the contents of the book.

L.C. classes theater as *dramatic representation* under literature (PN3200–); D.C. classes theater as *dramatic art* under amusements (792).

252 Moving pictures

(a) Works on the technique of making, projecting, and distribution of moving picture films: Class in mechanic trades or in photography according to system.

(b) Works on the history of moving pictures, on screen actors and actresses, or on photoplays: Class under theater.

(c) Works on the writing of photoplays or of script for the screen: Class as special topic under dramatic composition. Cf. Radio, (d) works on the writing of plays for broadcasting: 215d.

L.C. classes *moving picture shows* (PN1993), including scenario writing, under literature; D.C. classes scenario writing (808.2) in rhetoric.

(d) Works on moving pictures as used in education: Class in education.

L.C. classes visual education as a topic (LB1044) under pedagogics; D.C. does likewise (371.335).

253 Theatrical travel

Tours of theatrical persons: Class under their biography. E.g. *Henry Irving's impressions of America, narrated in a series of sketches, chronicles and conversations.* By Joseph Hatton (Boston, 1884). Class under biography of Henry Irving.

The reasons for this are: (1) interest centers in the person always; (2) the narrative deals with theatrical doings primarily, not with travel; (3) in case of doubt between a person and events in which he is concerned, choose the person.

The alternative rule given by the New York State Library: "Depends upon whether personal or travel element predominates," is difficult of application. The subject catalog will always supply the deficiencies of a rule consistently followed.

Example cited is classed by L.C. in description (E168) of the United States.

SPORTS

254 Hiking, climbing, camping, tours

(a) Works on the equipment and art of living in the open—clothing, camp utensils, woodcraft, and the like: Class in outdoor sports.—(Los Angeles). E.g. (1) *Going afoot, a book on walking.* [By] Bayard H. Christy (New York, 1920). (2) *Touring with tent and trailer.* By Winfield A. Kimball . . . (New York, 1937). (3) *Woodcraft.* [By George W. Sears] (New York, 1933). (4) *Camping out.* Ed. by Frank H. Cheley (New York, 1933).

Examples cited are classed: (1) by L.C. in walking (GV1071); so also by D.C. (796.51). (2) by L.C. in touring by automobile (GV1023); by D.C. in camping (796.54). (3) and (4) by L.C. in *camping* (SK601) under hunting sports; by D.C. in camping (796.54).

(b) Accounts of trips or of experiences in certain localities: Class in local travel. E.g. (1) *Hiking to Hamburg on $25.* By John P. Crawford [Bloomington, Ind., 1931]. (2)

Guide to Mexico for the motorist. [By] William Berlin Goolsby (Dallas, Tex., 1936).

Examples cited are classed: (1) by L.C. in voyages and travels (G470) ; so also by D.C. (910.4). (2) by L.C. in description (F1215) of Mexico; so also by D.C. (917.2).

LANGUAGE. PHILOLOGY

255 Definition and scope of the class

Philology as a science is closely associated with literature. Some languages are so remote from ordinary culture that the question arises whether works in these languages shall be classed as literature at all and not rather be treated as texts for the study of the language in which they are composed. The decision will depend largely on the type of library. Popular libraries ordinarily class foreign fiction in translation as if in English. Should they acquire other works in little known languages, they will prefer to treat them as linguistic texts. University and other libraries of research may consistently treat such languages as follows:

256 Foreign languages and literatures

(a) Works of the imagination, such as poetry, drama and fiction: Class by language.

(b) English translations of foreign fiction. See Translations: 30b.

(c) Selections, chrestomathies, and even single works, specially arranged for the study of the language in which they are printed: Class by language.

(d) Books of nonfiction in foreign languages: Class together by language in popular libraries, but by subject, without reference to the language, in reference, technical and university libraries. But cf. the special cases that follow.

(e) Specimens of dialects, patois and little-known literatures: Class by language, not by subject, in all libraries. E.g. Specimens of Basque, Italian dialects, American Indian, African and Oriental works (in the original) except versions of the Bible or its parts.

Catechisms in such languages are partly of religious and partly of philological interest; but only theological libraries will class catechisms printed in obscure languages under the subject. Translations of the Bible or of its parts into the less known languages are better kept together under Bible, but references should be made under the language in the subject catalog.

(f) The Bible or its parts in foreign versions: Class under Bible.

(g) Complete works of belles-lettres in the lesser known languages, e.g., Indic, Semitic and Hamitic: Class under those literatures.

As only libraries of research are likely to acquire such works, there is no reason for making exceptions.

(h) Liturgies in Oriental languages: Class in ritual.

(i) Literature of a religious sect written in an Oriental language: Class by topic. E.g. *The Sanskrit Buddhist literature of Nepal.* By Rájendralála Mitra (Calcutta, 1882). The subject of this analysis is Buddhism; the language is Sanskrit; the material, manuscript. Class by subject.

An alternative rule is: "Class all works by topic without regard to the language in which they are written, except in the case of the lesser known languages. Make language divisions under topics when necessary."—(Pettee).

Example cited is classed by L.C. in catalogs of manuscripts in libraries (Z6621.C13); by D.C. in bibliography of manuscripts (016.091) or in bibliography of Buddhism (016.2943).

(j) Translations into artificial languages. See Translations: 259b.

257 Foreign words or foreign constructions in a language

Class under the language *affected.* E.g. *Norse elements in English dialects.* By G. T. Flom (London, 1911). Class under English dialects.

Example cited is classed by L.C. in *Scandinavian words* (PE1582.S3) under English etymology.

258 Dictionaries of two languages

Dictionaries of two languages: Class under the foreign language if foreign-English; under the ancient language if ancient-modern; under the less generally known of two modern languages. In case of doubt, class under the language that is foreign to the country in which the dictionary appears. E.g. (1) C. E. Georges: *Dizionario latino-italiano; tr. con aggiunte condotta da Ferruccio Calonghi.* (2.ed.; Torino, 1913). Class under Latin. (2) *Dictionnaire italien-français de tous les (7852) verbes italiens.* Par V. Rossi-Sacchetti (Paris, 1909). Class under Italian.

259 Translations

The general treatment of translations is discussed under 30. Some special cases are the following:

(a) Extracts in translation from unfamiliar languages, brought together to illustrate a topic: Class under the topic. E.g. (1) *The wheel of the law; Buddhism illustrated from Siamese sources.* By Henry Alabaster (London, 1871). Class under Buddhism. (2) *Buddhism in Tibet illustrated by literary documents and objects of religious worship.* By Emil Schlagintweit, with tables in native print in the text. (Leipzig, 1863).

Examples cited are classed (1) by L.C. in Buddhism (BL1453). (2) by L.C. in *Lamaism* (BL1485) under Buddhism; so also by D.C. (294.32).

(b) Translations into artificial languages such as Esperanto or Volapük: Class with "readers" for students of that language, not with the originals. E.g. *Robinsono Kruso* [Robinson Crusoe in Esperanto]. (Philadelphia, 1908).

(c) Translations printed on alternate pages facing the original text: Class with translations, not with original texts. E.g. Loeb classical library.

LITERATURE

260 Definition and scope of the class

"The term literature is used by the classifications in the restricted sense of belles-lettres. If the distinction is drawn between the literature of the imagination and the literature of information, this subject group rigorously excludes the latter. Newman's *Idea of a university,* Burke's *Essay on the American revolution* are noble examples of literary masterpieces, but the material of these works, contributory to very definite topics of the subject classification, classes the books rather with a topic than with literature. As a general rule, a work of prose, whatever its claims to literary style, if it can be classed under a specific topic, has no place in literature. This restricts the class literature to (1) literary criticism, (2) literary history and biography, and (3) works of the imagination that fall under the various literary forms,—fiction, poetry, prose, etc."—(Pettee).

261 Criticism of one literature in another

Class under the literature *criticized.* E.g. *American literature in Spain.* By John De Lancey Ferguson. (New York, 1916). Class under American literature—History and criticism.

262 Quotations in ancient authors

(a) Quotations from ancient (classical) authors relating to a special topic: Class by topic, not in classics. E.g. *Ancient India as described in classical literature.* Tr. [and ed.] by J. W. McCrindle (Westminster, 1901). Class in history of India.

Example cited is classed by L.C. in history of India (DS451).

(b) Quotations taken from a single author or book, found in the works of an ancient author: Class under the author or work quoted. E.g. (1) *Philo and Holy Scripture; or, The quotations of Philo from the books of the Old Testament,* with intr. and notes by Herbert Edward Ryle (London, 1895). Class under Old Testament (Greek text). (2) *Philo von Alexandria als ausleger des Alten Testaments,* an sich selbst und nach seinem geschichtlichen einfluss betrachtet. (Jena, 1875).

Example (2) cited is classed by L.C. in *Philo* as a critic of the Old Testament (BS1161.P4).

263 **Periodical miscellany**

Literary essays, when issued in daily or weekly parts like the (old) *Spectator* or the *Tatler:* Class in literature (essays), not in periodicals.

This type of periodical is now nearly obsolete.

264 **Poetry and prose for public readings**

Collections of poetry or prose expressly designed for public readings: Class under oratory, not under the literary form, or in collections under the literature. E.g. *Choice readings for public and private entertainments.* By Robert McLean Cumnock (Chicago, 1924).

This conforms to the intent of the author and brings together a type of work that would otherwise be widely scattered.

HISTORY OF LITERATURE

265 **Influence of one literature upon another**

Class under the literature *affected.* E.g. (1) The influence of Old Norse literature upon English literature. Influence of India and Persia on the poetry of Germany. Greek influence on English poetry. Influence of Italian upon French literature. Influence of the French revolution upon Italian literature. (2) *The Greek romances in Elizabethan prose fiction.* By S. L. Wolff (New York, 1912). Class under history of English fiction. But (3) *Early influence of German literature in America.* By Frederick H. Wilkens (New York, n.d.). Class under German literature in *America,* not with American literature or American writers as influenced by German models.

An additional consideration is that one literature influencing another literature is practically a source of the material and forms used in the latter, and sources should be classed under the subject to which they have furnished material.

L.C. classes this type of work under *relations* (of each literature) to foreign literatures, e.g. relation of Norse to English literature (PR129.N8) under English literature; of French to Italian literature (PQ4050.F5) under the Italian. Examples cited are classed

by L.C. (2) as topic (PR839.G7) under English fiction, (3) as topic (PT123.U6) under German literature.
Cf. Literary influence: 281.

266 Animals as subjects in literature

(a) Stories of animals, birds, insects, and the like, when written for children: Class in the same way as other children's literature. Cf. Children: 35.

(b) Popular scientific works on animals: Class in natural history.

(c) Literary treatment of animals by famous authors (e.g. Dante) : Class in criticism of that author.

(d) Literary treatment of animals in a special literature: Class in literary history of that literature.

267 Author's opinions as subjects in literature

While works treating of an author or of his works will be classed under that author, his own opinions upon certain topics will not necessarily be classed with the rest of his writings. E.g. *Wordsworth's literary criticism;* extracts ed. with an introduction by Nowell C. Smith (London, 1905). Class under literary criticism, not with Wordsworth's individual works (unless system puts all there). The author catalog will bring out the personal element, leaving the subjects upon which Wordsworth has written to be brought out by the subject catalog. Wordsworth's *Guide to the lakes* is still less personal and will be classed in description. Cf. Works of philosophers: 67d; also Personal opinions: 346b–c.

L.C. classes all of Wordsworth's works together (PR5850–) under individual English authors.

268 Persons as subjects in literature

(a) Works about heroes of romance or poetry: Class in literature, even though the persons are historic, i.e. King Arthur, Charlemagne. E.g. *Legends of Charlemagne; or, Romance of the middle ages.* By Thomas Bulfinch (Boston, 1867).

Example cited is classed: by L.C. in *legends of Charlemagne* (PN687.C5) under general literature; by D.C. in *legends* (398.22) under folklore.

(b) Works on literary "characters": Class as literature whether the characters are fictitious or real persons. E.g. *The legend of fair Helen as told by Homer, Goethe and others.* By Eugene Oswald (New York, 1905).

Mythological characters figuring in literature are to be classed under the literature in which they figure, not under the religion in which they first appear.

Example cited is classed by L.C. (PN57.H4) in individual characters in literature.

269 Philosophy as a subject in literature

Philosophic doctrines and ideas as introduced into poetry or other literary forms: Class in literature. E.g. Studies in the philosophy of the Meistersingers, i.e. scholasticism as it appears in the German poetry of their time. A work of literary criticism, not on philosophy, because the literature is the subject affected. Analogously a work on the influence of scholasticism on German medieval poetry would be classed under literature. Treatment of "influence on," "topic appearing in," and "effect of," is similar.

270 Things as subjects treated in literature

Literary history of a particular subject as treated in literature: Class in literature if the topic is one that can be brought out there; otherwise under the subject. E.g. (1) *Six lectures on the recorder and other flutes in relation to literature.* By C. Welch (London, 1911). Class under flute. (2) *Precious stones in Old English literature.* By Robert Max Garrett (Leipzig, 1909). Class under Old English literature, not under precious stones (in art).

The rule should be interpreted to imply literary and not specific treatment of the object. The subject catalog will, of course, bring out all works treating of the thing in question.

Examples cited are classed: (1) by L.C. in *flute* (ML935) under musical literature. (2) by L.C. in series (Münchener beiträge zur romanischen und englischen philologie), but L.C. has subhead *treatment of special subjects* under literatures.

Cf. Subjects treated in poetry: 275; Animals as subjects in literature: 266.

POETRY

271 Chronicles in verse

Class in poetry.

It is impracticable for the classifier to attempt to decide that one chronicle in verse is more valuable as history than as literature, and another is more poetry than history. Once the classifier begins to class poetry, however lacking in literary importance, by the subject, he gets into difficulties and inconsistencies.

272 Metrical translations

(a) If the original is poetry: Class with the original. E.g. Chapman's translation of Homer.

(b) If the translation is so free that the original is related to it merely as a source: Class as a poem by the translator. E.g. Sir Thomas Malory's "Le morte d'Arthur."

(c) If the language of the translation has more interest in itself than the subject matter: Class as a text in that language. E.g. King Alfred's Anglo-Saxon version of Pope Gregory the Great's *Pastoral rule.*

273 Philosophy in poetry

A work on philosophy or philosophic ideas in the poets: Class in literary history. E.g. (1) *Of philosophy in the poets.* By James Hutchinson Stirling (Edinburgh, 1885). (2) *National and international ideals in the English poets.* By C. H. Herford (Manchester, 1916).

The reason for this is that the poetic treatment of philosophic ideas is closer akin to poetry than to philosophy.

274 Poems on persons (Collections)

(a) Anthologies of poems on persons (not literary): Class with biography of the person. E.g. *The praise of Lincoln, an anthology.* Collected and arranged by A. Dallas Williams (Indianapolis, 1911).

(b) Anthologies of poems in praise of poets and other

writers: Class with criticism of their works. E.g. Dante; Shakespeare.

275 Subjects treated in poetry

Class in poetry, subdivided by themes, if desired. E.g. *Sea songs and ballads.* Selected by Christopher Stone (Oxford, 1906).

Topics treated in poetry should be classed under poetry on the principle that poetry is seldom considered as literature of information.

Example cited is classed by L.C. in *sea* as topic (PN6110.S4) under poetry.

Cf. Poems on persons: 274.

DRAMA

276 Drama

(a) Drama dealing with a special topic or written for a special occasion: Class under drama, not by subject. E.g. *Depositio cornuti typographici, that is, a play which can be performed at the reception and confirmation of journeymen.* (New York, 1911). Class in drama.

To class plays according to the occasion for which they are written will be difficult to do consistently; it is better to let the catalog bring out the subjects treated in drama. Cf. Pageants: 170.

Example cited is classed by L.C. (Z123) under printing. D.C. classes school plays (371.895) under education.

(b) Historical plays: Class under drama of the literature in which written. E.g. *English historical plays by Shakespeare, Marlowe, Peele, Heywood, Fletcher and Ford,* arranged for acting as well as for reading. By Thomas Donovan (London, 1896. 2v.). Class in English drama.

The subject catalog will bring out their relation to history, if worth while.

(c) Plays arranged for acting: Class in drama of the literature in which written, not under theater. But class plays written especially for amateurs under acting.

Only in special theatrical libraries or in special collections of general libraries, class in theater (acting). L.C. classes *plays for ama-*

teurs (PN6120–) under general literature (only) ; D.C. in private theatricals (793.1).

(d) Prose rendering of plays or poems of individual authors: Class with the originals. E.g. (1) Lamb's *Tales from Shakespeare.* (2) *Stories from The earthly paradise.* By William Morris, retold in prose by C. S. Evans (London, 1915).

In a juvenile collection such tales would be classed with stories for children.
Examples cited are classed by L.C. (1) in *paraphrases* (PR2877) under Shakespeare. (2) in English fiction (PZ8.1).

(e) Texts of dramas, prepared for students of the language by the addition of notes and vocabulary: Class with "readers" and texts for the study of the language.—(Queens Borough). E.g. Molière's *Le bourgeois gentilhomme.* Ed. with intr., notes [and vocabulary] by F. M. Warren (Boston, 1899). Class under French language, not with other dramas of Molière. The author catalog will of course bring out such editions of a given author. Cf. Foreign languages and literatures : 256c.

(f) Dramatic adaptations of works of fiction: Class under drama. E.g. Dickens' *Christmas carol* arranged for the stage or for radio broadcasting.

An alternative is to put in drama only adaptations in which the language is considerably changed as, e.g. (1) Boucicault's play *Rip Van Winkle* based on Irving's story; (2) many photoplays based upon novels.
If system classes plays with other works of an individual author, not in drama, dramatic adaptations will be classed with the original work.

ESSAYS

277 Essays

(a) Essays, whether by one or by several writers, treating of a specific subject: Class under the topic, not with other essays in literature. E.g. *Essays in the study of Sienese painting.* By Bernard Berenson (New York, 1918). Class in painting.

(b) A collection of essays on several subjects: Class in essays of the literature in which written.

(c) Critical and literary essays dealing with writers of a special literature or period: Class under the literary history of that period. E.g. *Select essays of Sainte-Beuve, chiefly bearing on English literature.* Tr. by A. J. Butler (London, n.d.). Class in English literary history, not with works of the French author.

The alternative of classing all essays as a form of literature sacrifices the needs of the student to the convenience of the reader for recreation. An essay may be as informing as a treatise.

Example cited is classed by L.C. with other works of Sainte-Beuve (PQ2391.A15) under French literature.

(d) Single essays: Class by subject.

LITERARY CRITICISM

278 Literary criticism

Criticism of literary critics: Class with literary history. E.g. *The masters of French criticism.* By Irving Babbitt (Boston, 1912). Class under French literary history.

279 Literary topography

(a) Literary history of a place, including literary associations of buildings and streets: Class in literature, not in description or history. E.g. *Literary landmarks of London.* By Laurence Hutton (4th ed.; Boston, 1888).

Example cited is classed by L.C. in *literary landmarks* of London (PR110.L6) under English literature.

(b) A work written expressly to illustrate the life and works of an author by description of places associated with him: Class with works about that author. E.g. (1) *Shakespeare's England, an account of the life and manners of his age.* (Oxford, 1917. 2v.). (2) *The land of Burns, a series of landscapes and portraits illustrative of the life and writings of the Scottish poet.* (Glasgow, 1840. 2v.). (3) *The Wessex of Thomas Hardy.* By Sir B. C. A. Windle (London, 1902).

Examples cited are classed: (1) by L.C. in *age of Shakespeare* (PR2910) under Shakespeare. (2) by L.C. in *landmarks and haunts* of Robert Burns (PR4334) under his writings. (3) by L.C. in *Dorsetshire* (DA670.D7) under description.

(c) Literary associations of a place. See Literary shrines: 314a. Cf. Historic houses: 319b.

280 Literature vs. Archeology

An archeological work illustrative of an ancient author: Class with literature about that author. E.g. *Troy, a study in Homeric geography*. By Walter Leaf (London, 1912). "Essay which aims at testing the tradition of the Trojan War by comparing the text of Homer with the natural conditions described . . . in the Iliad." Class under Homer.

If the intent of the author is to illumine the text by archeological finds, the work should be classed with commentaries on that author. If, on the other hand, archeology is the intent, class under archeology.

281 Literary influence

(a) Influence of several writers upon a literature: Class under the literature affected. E.g. *Corneille and Racine in England . . . the English translations . . . with especial reference to their presentation on the English stage*. By Dorothea F. Canfield (New York, 1904). Class under English dramatic history.

(b) Influence of one writer upon another. See this heading under Individual authors: 292b.

(c) Reaction against influence; absence of certain influences or the reaction against them: Class the same as influence. E.g. (1) The revolt of romantic drama against the classical tradition of the three dramatic unities. Class under general, not Greek, drama. (2) *The reaction against metaphysics in theology*. By Douglas Clyde Macintosh (Chicago, 1911). Class in theology.

Examples cited are classed by L.C. (1) in *technique* (PN1672) under general drama. (2) in philosophy of doctrinal theology (BT40).

(d) Influence of one literature upon another. See 265.

282 Race publications

Books written by authors of one race, e.g. Negroes. Class by topic. E.g. *The Afro-American press and its editors.* By I. G. Penn (Springfield, Mass., 1891). Class under bibliography of newspapers; the subject catalog will bring out its relation to Negroes.

The alternative of classing together all works written by Negroes will bring out the feature of Negro literary achievements; but this aspect of the Negro question may better be left to the subject catalog.

Example cited is classed by L.C. in *Negro press* (PN4888.N4) under journalism.

INDIVIDUAL AUTHORS

283 Definition

Individual authors, as the term is used in library technique, means authors writing in the field of belles-lettres, e.g. drama or poetry, as distinguished from those contributing to the literature of information. Such writers are often the subject of literary or artistic criticism, directed at them individually, in a way that other writers are not.

284 Arrangement of works of individual authors

Class together by literature, either by authors divided into periods, or in that form of literature (drama, essays, poetry) to which most of a given author's writings belong. E.g. Tennyson's poems, dramas, and collected editions of his works. Do not separate, putting his poems in English poetry, his plays in English drama and his collected works apart from his poems.

Works of belles-lettres are not like literature of information, important for the subject; separation of form may perplex the classifier and be of slight value to the student of literature.

D.C. separates the works of individual authors in belles-lettres by form; e.g. the name of Oliver Goldsmith appears under 18th century English poetry, 18th century English fiction, and 18th century English essays, the location under fiction being emphasized. L.C. divides the authors under each literature by period and keeps all of their works together, often by detailed schemes; Goldsmith appears under the period 1640–1770. Cutter advises keeping all the works of an author together.

285 Author's nationality vs. language

In literature consider the language used by the writer, and class by that, disregarding the country of the author's birth or residence.

Thus British writers using Norman French, or French or Italian writers using medieval Latin are to be classed by literature, not by nationality.

(a) If the author writes only in Latin (medieval or modern): Class in Latin (medieval or modern). E.g. *The eclogues of Baptista Mantuanus* (Baltimore, 1911). Class this Italian writer under medieval Latin literature.

(b) If he writes in both the Latin and the vernacular: Class by the vernacular. E.g. Milton, Bacon.

(c) If he writes in several languages (modern): Class by his nationality.—(Pettee).

286 Criticism of individual authors

(a) Critical works about an author's writings: Class in literature, unless a special scheme is used under biography; but do not separate by kind. E.g. *The classical mythology of Milton's English poems.* By Charles Grosvenor Osgood (New York, 1900).

If literature is preferred, group the critical works near the collected works of the author. Do not class works upon an author's prose in one place and upon his poetry in another.

(b) Criticism of a single work of an author: Class next to the editions of the work. E.g. *The "Samson Agonistes" of Milton.* By J. M. Brown (Christchurch, n.d.).

(c) Criticism of a translator's collective work: Class under his name as in rule above; but criticism of a single translation made by him class with other works upon the original author. E.g. Criticisms of Pope's "Homer." Class next to the translation, under Homer.

As no classification will group together all the translations made by a given translator; so no classification can bring under a translator all the criticism of his translations. The subject catalog must do that.

287 Dictionaries of individual authors

(a) A dictionary of the language of an individual author: Class with other works about that author, not with other dictionaries of the language used by that author. E.g. *Schopenhauer-Lexikon* . . . bearbeitet von Julius Frauenstädt (Leipzig, 1871. 2v.). Class under Schopenhauer, in philosophy.

(b) A dictionary of the characters and scenes occurring in the works of an author: Class with the works of that author. E.g. *A Dickens dictionary, the characters and scenes.* By Alex Philip (London, 1909).

288 Knowledge of a special subject possessed and exhibited by an author

(a) If the author writes professedly upon the subject: Class by subject.

In this case a work upon the author's knowledge is practically a review of his work.

(b) If the author writes belles-lettres in which the subject appears incidentally: Class in literary criticism of the author. E.g. (1) *Milton's knowledge of music.* By Sigmund Gottfried Spaeth (Princeton, 1913). (2) Shakespeare's knowledge of law, music, etc.

L.C. has topic *treatment and knowledge of special subjects* under individual authors; D.C. has topic *learning* (F).

289 Literary comparison and relation

(a) Comparison of the work of two writers: Class under the writer supposed to be influenced or deriving material from the other. E.g. *Euripides and Shaw with other essays.* By Gilbert Norwood (Boston, 1921). Class under Shaw.

In the case of writers living at different periods, the one influenced will obviously be the later writer.

Example cited is classed by L.C.—perhaps because of the "other essays"—in history of the drama (PN1721).

Cf. Influence: 292b.

(b) Relation of an author to his time or to literature:
Class under literary criticism of that author. E.g. *Spenser's
"Shepherd's calendar" in relation to contemporary affairs.*
By J. J. Higginson (New York, 1912). Class with works
on Spenser's writings.

(c) Works compared one with another: Class under the
work of the literature intended by the author to be illustrated by the comparison. E.g. *Piers Plowman, a comparison with some earlier and contemporary French allegories.*
By Dorothy L. Owen (London, 1912). Class with "Piers
Plowman."

**290 Literary history of an individual author in the form of
references, criticism or appreciations relating to him**

Class under the author concerned. E.g. *The praise of
Shakespeare, an English anthology.* Comp. by C. E. Hughes
(London, 1904). While no classifier would hesitate to class
this book under Shakespeare, other analogous cases are not
so obvious.

291 Literary illustration of an author

Contemporary sociological, political, or other conditions
illustrating an author's work: Class with literary criticism
of the author. E.g. *Homeric society; a sociological study of
the Iliad and Odyssey.* By Albert Galloway Keller (New
York, 1911). Class with the literature on Homer, although
its subject matter is sociological, because the intent of the
author is to illustrate Homer's works.

292 Literary influence of individual writers

(a) Influence of a writer upon a literature: Class with
the literary criticism of the author concerned. E.g. (1)
*Moore en France . . . œuvres de Thomas Moore dans la
littérature française, 1819–1839.* Par A. B. Thomas (Paris,
1911). Class under Moore, as it is restricted to the fortunes
of Moore's works in French translations and imitations.
(2) *The influence of Baudelaire in France and England.* By
G. Turquet-Milnes (London, 1913). Class under Baude-

laire. (3) *The influence of Molière on Restoration comedy.*
By D. H. Miles (New York, 1910). Class under works on
Molière (literary history).

Examples (1) and (2) are classed by L.C. as in above rule; (3)
in *Restoration* period (PR695) under English drama.

These examples, it will be noted, show that in the case of individual
influence the rule is opposite to the rule concerning the influence of
one literature or event upon another. The justification for this apparent inconsistency lies in the greater importance of persons. What
concerns them individually should be kept together; the individual
outweighs the thing. If the topic or event concerned is definite and
precise, some classifiers may prefer to class under it. E.g. Cardinal
Aleman and the Great Schism. But one would hardly class *Talleyrand et la société européenne,* by Frédéric Loliée (Paris, 1911) under
European society.

(b) Influence of one writer upon another: Class under
the writer influenced or affected. E.g. (1) *Walter Paget's
einfluss auf Oscar Wilde.* Von Eduard J. Bock (Bonn,
1913). Class under Wilde, if this series (Bonner Studien
. . .) is scattered. (2) *Dante & Aquinas.* By Philip H.
Wicksteed (London, 1913). Class under Dante. (3) *Tennyson and Virgil; an essay on the indebtedness of Tennyson
to Virgil.* Class with Tennyson, as the author affected.

Examples cited are classed by L.C. (1) in *imitations* (PR5824)
under Wilde. (2) in *sources* (PQ4417) under Dante. (3) in *sources*
(PR5586) under Tennyson.

293 Literary sources

(a) Sources of an author's work: Class under that
author, not under the source, even when the source is a
single book. E.g. *Râma and Homer; an argument that in
the Indian epics Homer found the theme of his two great
poems.* By Arthur Lillie (London, 1912). Class under
Homer.

Example cited is classed by L.C. in *comparative studies* (PA4052)
under Homer.

(b) Source of an individual literary work, plot or story:
Class under the work derived, not under the source. E.g.
Faust and the Clementine recognitions. By E. C. Richard-

son (1894). Class under Faust legend. Cf. Influence: 292b.

(c) An individual work treated as the source of another work and compared throughout with it: Class with the latter work, especially historical sources used in literature. E.g. *Shakespeare's Holinshed. The chronicle and the historical plays compared.* By W. G. Boswell-Stone. (2d ed.; London, 1907). Class under Shakespeare.

The intent of the editor of the source is to illustrate the later work and the parallel passages from the source, introduced by the editor into his edition, essentially differentiate it from other editions of the source.

L.C. classes as *sources* (PR2955) under Shakespeare such authors as Holinshed, Lyly, Montaigne, Plutarch.

(d) An individual work, though known to be the source of another but not compared with it and not annotated as such. Class under its own subject. E.g. Other editions of Holinshed's *Chronicle.* Class under history of England.

To class every edition, e.g. of a given chronicle, under Shakespeare merely because he used it, would manifestly be absurd.

The subject catalog will make the necessary references. The rule would be modified for special collections.

Literary topography. See Literary topography: 279.

294 Philosophy of individual writers

Philosophy (i.e. the metaphysical or ethical system) of a writer of belles-lettres: Class in literary criticism of that author. E.g. Dante; Shakespeare.

This may seem inconsistent with our rule Works of philosophers: (67d) to class views of philosophers, upon topics other than philosophic, by topic. But philosophers write informational literature; philosophy of writers of belles-lettres is rather of critical interest.

Cf. Philosophic ideas in literature: 68.

HISTORY

295 Scope and definition of the class

"The term history in its amplest meaning includes every vestige of everything that has happened to man since he first appeared, and the tendency of recent historical writers is to emphasize less the purely political events and to select significant events in all phases of human affairs. The classifications, however, keep to the more restricted definition of history, and limit the class strictly to the general development of political units and their parts, gathering here, along with the history of national units, various groups of material of a general nature contributory to this history, such as biography, genealogy, geography, archeology, diplomatics, etc.

"By the definition of history as the record of the development of racial or political units, *as a whole,* development of human progress along *special lines* is barred from this class. Only material on movements or events affecting the state as a whole have a place in this class. History of special phases of national life, e.g. church history, economic history, are classed with these special subjects, not with the general class History. If it is desired to include in the class History special phases of national development, the classifications can readily be modified to permit this. Cutter has provided for this. Columbia university and Vassar college have both worked out schemes which are used with the Dewey."— (Pettee).

296 Conspiracies and plots

History of a conspiracy or plot: Class under the history of the country or under the topic, not under biography of the conspirator or leader of the plot. E.g. Catiline's conspiracy.

Example cited is classed by L.C. in Rome, period B.C. 111–78 (DG259).

297 Economics vs. History

(a) Works treating of economic conditions or movements: Class in economic history. E.g. *Economic and social conditions in France during the eighteenth century.* By Henri Sée; tr. by E. H. Zeydell (New York, 1927).

(b) Works treating of historical events that may have owed their origin or progress to economic causes: Class in history. E.g. (1) Wat Tyler's insurrection; (2) Gordon riots.

298 Government vs. History

A historical narrative, written to exhibit the application of certain principles in the government of a country: Class under history unless these principles are of very specific character. E.g. *Peace principles exemplified in the early history of Pennsylvania*. By Samuel M. Janney (Philadelphia, 1888). Class under history of Pennsylvania.

See also History of political ideas vs. History of events: 300.

"If the book is written to illustrate the development of these principles, class with the topic where the principles belong; if it is to show how the history of the country was modified by these principles, class in history. E.g. A work on the working of local option in a definite place would go under the temperance movement unless it was the intention of the author to write a town history in which the general trend of events had been affected by local option."—(Pettee).

299 Historical traditions embodied in literature

Works tracing the record of historical events in certain works of literature, e.g. poetry: Class in history. E.g. *Sidelights on Teutonic history during the migration period*. By M. G. Clarke (Cambridge, 1911). Studies from "Beowulf" and other Old English poems, but primarily a contribution to history, not to literature.

300 History of political ideas vs. History of events

(a) History of a political idea, like liberty or patriotism: Class with other works on the idea.

(b) History of *events* illustrating a political idea or principle: Class under history of the events. E.g. (1) *The history of English patriotism*. By Esmé Wingfield-Stratford (London, 1913. 2v.). Classed best under social history of England. (2) *French patriotism in the nineteenth century, 1814-1833*. By H. F. Stewart and Paul Desjardins (Cambridge, 1923). Class in French history.

The reason lies: (1) in the difficulty of distinguishing history of the idea as such from history of events; (2) in the fact that, as a rule, such a work treats, not of the idea as such, but of events caused or promoted by the idea.

301 Patriotic society publications

(a) Reports and lists of members of patriotic societies: Class under the societies (Revolution, Colonial wars, and the like).

(b) Other publications of these societies: Class by subject, as the society acts merely as editor. E.g. *Information for immigrants* . . . prepared by the National Society of the Sons of the American Revolution (Washington, 1908). Class under citizenship.

Example cited is classed by L.C. in *advice to immigrants* (JV6543) under immigration and the state.

302 Political history

Class in history.

Political history is both a history of discussion and a record of events. The distinction between political and general history of a country is one not of method but of relative emphasis. Hence political history may be looked upon as a special form of writing history. History of political parties, however, is a history of politics.

303 Politics

Distinguish between politics and history.

Politics is discussion, argument, documents and the like, bearing upon measures, policies and movements contemporaneous with the writing of the books or pamphlets in which these movements are discussed. History is the record of the events after they have occurred. History of the discussions themselves is either bibliography or political history, according to the make-up of the book. Classifiers who prefer to class all contemporary discussions of political policies under history will do well to place them under sub-headings rather than mix them with narrative history. L.C. classes campaign literature, pamphlets, political tracts and the like, by period under the history of the country or state.

304 Source material for history

(a) Source books written professedly to furnish a collection of historical material of varied character relating to the history of some country or period: Class in history, whatever the form of the material. E.g. *Source book of English history*. Ed. by Elizabeth Kimball Kendall (New

York, 1912). Includes extracts from chronicles, diaries. trials, poems.

(b) Books upon the history of a country or period considered from some special point of view—economic, social, artistic or literary: Class by topic. E.g. (1) *Tudor economic documents.* Ed. by R. H. Tawney and Eileen Power (London, 1924. 3v.). Class in economic history of England. (2) *Historical aspects of the immigration problem, select documents.* By Edith Abbott (Chicago, 1926). Class under immigration.

(c) Contemporary speeches, tracts or other discussions of a political character: Class in politics; or if placed in history, separate from narrative histories of the country or period.

It is true that such material is valuable to the historian and student of history. But so is everything that has had influence in shaping the history of a nation. On the other hand, the student of economics has first claim to works treating primarily of the history of his subject, and only partially of the general history of a country. But contemporaneous political tracts, discussions, arguments and documents are more closely related to politics than to history.

"Treat as sources of history, classing with history, collections of charters, contemporary letters or other writings when such material is brought together primarily to illustrate an historical topic."— (Pettee).

(d) Documentation, used here in the sense of the value, method of using, and recording of documents as source material: Class in historiography. E.g. (1) *History as a science.* By Mohini Mohan Chatterji (London, 1927). (2) *Some thoughts on recent methods of historical research.* By W. B. Boyd-Carpenter (1924). (3) *Masters' essays in history, a manual of instructions.* By Allan Nevins (New York, 1933).

(e) Documentation in the sense of bibliography: Class in bibliography. E.g. Reports of the World Congress of Universal Documentation, Paris, 1937.

(f) Diplomatics or use of documents in the study of writing at different periods, or of writing as evidence of authenticity: Class in paleography. E.g. (1) *Palæography and the practical study of court hand.* By Hilary Jenkinson (Cambridge, 1915). (2) *Palæography; notes upon the history of writing and the medieval art of illumination.* By Bernard Quaritch (London, 1894).

(g) Works on government documents as sources of information: Class in national bibliography. E.g. *United States government publications as sources of information for libraries.* By Anne Morris Boyd (New York, 1931).

305 Reigns and centuries

(a) A historical work covering three or more reigns or administrations: Class under the century or other inclusive period. E.g. *Monstrelet's chronicles 1400–1467 (1516).* (London, 1809. 5v.). Class under Valois.

(b) If the period covers two reigns: Class under the first reign. E.g. *Chronique des règnes de Jean II* [1350–1364] *et de Charles V* [1364–1380] (Paris, 1910). Class under John II.

(c) If the intention of the author is to treat one or the other reign primarily: Class under that. E.g. *France under Mazarin with a review of the administration of Richelieu.* By James Breck Perkins (New York, 1902. 2v.). Class under Louis XIV.

The New York State Library rule is: "If not more than three reigns are covered, class under the first or most important (from the standpoint of the treatment) unless three cover more than half of the more inclusive division."

Example cited is classed by L.C. in reign of Louis XIII (DC123).

306 Revolutions

(a) Events of a period preceding a revolution: Class under the actual period covered. E.g. Taine's *Ancien régime.* Should be classed in French history *before* the Revolution.

(b) When the intent of the author is to treat the revolution and its antecedent causes: Class under the revolution. E.g. *England and America 1763–1783: the history of a re-*

action. By Mary A. M. Marks (London, 1907. 2v.). Treats
of events in America and England leading up to and *including* the American revolution and should be classed under
that.

307 Social culture and civilization

(a) Works on civilization in general—its theory, values,
elements, group phenomena, social institutions: Class in
sociology.—(Los Angeles). E.g. (1) *Principles of western civilisation.* By Benjamin Kidd (New York, 1902).
(2) *Readings in the story of human progress.* Ed. by Leon
C. Marshall (New York, 1926).

(b) Works on the history of civilization, treated chrono-
logically: Class in history.—(Los Angeles). E.g. (1) *The
history of western civilization.* By Harry Elmer Barnes
New York, 1935–). (2) *Civilization in the making.*
By Millard S. Everett . . . (Chicago, 1935). (3) *Whither
mankind, a panorama of modern civilization.* Ed. by Charles
A. Beard (New York, 1934). (4) *History of ancient civilization.* By Albert A. Trever (New York, 1936).

(c) Works on the civilization of individual countries:
Class in history of the country. E.g. (1) *The civilization of
France.* By Ernst Robert Curtius; tr. by Olive Wyon (New
York, 1932). (2) *Old world origins of American civiliza-
tion.* By James J. Reynolds . . . (New York, 1934).

(d) When several countries are concerned: Class under
a larger inclusive heading, e.g. Europe, Orient, Roman empire, British empire, in history. E.g. (1) *The civilizations of
the east.* By René Grousset; tr. by Catherine Alison Phillips
(London, 1931–34. 4v.). (2) *Modern European civilization.* By Roscoe Lewis Ashley (New York, 1918). (3) *A
cultural history of the modern age.* By Egon Friedell; tr.
by Charles Francis Atkinson (New York, 1930–32. 3v.).

308 Social history of a reign or period

Class under the history of that reign or period, in preference to mixing such works with social history of the country
in general. E.g. (1) *The great days of Versailles; studies*

from court life in the later years of Louis XIV. By G. F.
Bradby (New York, 1906). Class under Louis XIV. (2)
Social France at the time of Philip Augustus. By Achille
Luchaire; tr. by E. B. Krehbiel (New York, 1912). Class
under reign of Philip Augustus.

309 Time divisions vs. Local divisions

"There seems to be no uniformity of practice here. It
would seem worth while to make some rigid rulings and adhere to them consistently. In general, local divisions seem
to take precedence over time divisions. The history of Virginia in colonial times is usually classed with the history of
Virginia, not with the general history of the colonial period
of United States history. It seems in the line of general
usage to suggest a ruling that all periods in the history
of definite localities be classed as local history, e.g. that
A. R. Bayley's *The great civil war in Dorset, 1642–1660*
(Taunton, 1910) go with Dorset. Of course a bit of local
history that is treated, not as local history, but as an incident
in the general history of the times, is different and should
go with general history. *Robert Kett and the Norfolk
rising*, by Joseph Clayton (London, 1912) is an illustration
of this kind. A rigid adherence to this ruling would scatter
the histories of the Reformation into the periods of church
history under the various countries, but this, in my opinion,
is desirable."—(Pettee).

Cf. Time divisions (in general) : 39–41.

The essential point is that local treatment of history should be
brought out under its proper heading in the classification, either in
local history as such or in local subdivision under the sections devoted
to wars or other events. Such books should not be classed, alphabetically by author, in the same section as general histories of these
events, for to do so is to bury them, so far as classification is concerned.

(a) History of local events which concern only local affairs (government, people or place) : Class in local history.

(b) History of local events which formed part of national
movements (revolutions, insurrections, military opera-

tions) : Class in national history by period or under the war of which they formed incidents. E.g. Boston massacre; War of La Vendée.

(c) History of a city or town during the period of a war: Class by history of the place. E.g. (1) *Groton during the Indian wars.* By Samuel A. Green (Groton, Mass., 1883). (2) *Groton during the Revolution.* By Samuel A. Green (Groton, 1900). Class both in local history.

(d) Local risings in which one section only of a country is concerned: Class under the local history of that country, i.e. under the scene of operations. E.g. *The story of Bacon's rebellion.* By Mary Newton Stanard (New York, 1907). Class under history of Virginia, not under Colonial history of the United States.

The line is not always easy to draw; but the system will provide for all important revolutions.

(e) Local risings that formed part of national movements: Class with those movements, after the analogy of battles and campaigns of a war. E.g. (1) *Robert Kett and the Norfolk rising.* By Joseph Clayton (London, 1912). Class under reign of Edward VI (unless placed under biography of Kett), because this rising was only one of several. (2) *The great revolt of 1381* [i.e. Wat Tyler's insurrection in East Anglia]. By Charles Oman (Oxford, 1906). Class under reign of Richard II. (3) *The great civil war in Dorset, 1642–1660.* By A. R. Bayley (Taunton, 1910). Class under Puritan period, 1642–1660. But cf. Miss Pettee's note (p.139).

Revolutions involving dependent *countries,* like Ireland or the Netherlands while under Spanish rule, will of course be classed under the country.

TRAVEL AND DESCRIPTION

310 Travel and description

(a) Personal accounts of travel: Class with other description of the places visited.

(b) In the case of distinguished travelers, like royalty

and famous generals, whose personality may be of more interest than the scenes described: Class in biography of the person. E.g. *Around the world with General Grant.* By John Russell Young (New York, 1879. 2v.). Class in biography of Grant.

Example cited is classed by L.C. in tours around the world (G440).

(c) Travels undertaken professedly for research along definite lines, e.g. epigraphy, antiquities, bibliography: Class by topic treated. E.g. *An epigraphical journey in Asia Minor.* By J. R. S. Sterrett (Boston, 1888). Class in inscriptions. (2) *A bibliographical . . . tour in France and Germany.* By T. F. Dibdin (London). Class in bibliography. Cf. Scientific expeditions: 176.

(d) Encyclopedic works treating of countries in a general way, differing from works of travel, wider than government and institutions, more literary and less mathematical than statistics: Class as local encyclopedias. E.g. (1) *Japan by the Japanese.* Ed. by Alfred Stead (New York, 1904). (2) *The Mexican year book* (Los Angeles, 1922–   ).

The New York State Library, as also D.C., classes this type of book in description. The objection to this treatment is that it puts the book along with works of travel, which are quite different in purpose, form and contents. L.C. has heading *comprehensive works* under countries in classes D, E, F.

Examples cited are classed by L.C. (1) in description of Japan (DS810). (2) under history of Mexico (F1208).

311 Biblical geography

Biblical geography, as used here, is description, identification and the like, of places mentioned in the Bible, with reference to the elucidation of the Bible; it does not mean geography of Palestine or of other countries irrespective of connection with Biblical events. Identification of places mentioned in the Bible may go under Bible. Only a theological library will construe present-day travel in Bible lands as illustrative only of the Bible.

Travel in Palestine and other Bible regions: Class in travel. E.g. *The immovable East; studies of the people and customs of Palestine.* By Philip J. Baldensperger (London, 1913). Class in travel.

Example cited is classed by L.C. in *social life* of Palestine (DS112) under history.

312 Explorations

Treat broadly the localities visited on voyages of discovery or travels of exploration.

Such regions as America, the East and West Indies, or the Orient, may be treated very partially in early works on them. Yet these early descriptions are the only ones there are of these regions at that time. A safe rule is to follow broadly the title and trend of the book, and not class as local, accounts treating of a period before settlements have been made in a region and local history has begun. Examples of loose nomenclature are "America," the "West Indies," and "East Indies."

313 History of local travel

(a) Books of reminiscence or history of old-time travel: Class under travel unless they include also considerable local history. E.g. *Across the plains in '65; a youngster's journal.* [By Francis Crissey Young] (Denver, 1905). Class in travel in the West.

(b) Early history of rivers (i.e. steamboats, piloting, etc.): Class under history of travel. E.g. *Old times on the upper Mississippi; the recollections of a steamboat pilot from 1854 to 1863.* By G. B. Merrick (Cleveland, 1909). Class under travel on the Mississippi.

New York State Library classes under transportation. L.C. classes the example in history of the Northwest (F597).

(c) History of a river and of the neighboring region: Class in history of the region. E.g. *60 years on the upper Mississippi; my life and experiences.* By S. W. McMaster (Rock Island [1895]). Class in history of the Mississippi Valley.

Example cited is classed by L.C. in history of the Northwest (F597).

314 Literary shrines

(a) Works on shrines, coffee-houses, inns and other haunts of authors: Class as topic under biography of

authors. E.g. *Some literary associations of East Anglia.* By
William A. Dutt (New York, 1907).

> L.C. classes literary landmarks, homes and haunts of authors as
> topic in history of each literature, or under individual writers.

(b) Works on historic houses and buildings associated
with historical events. See Historic houses: 319.

315 Place names beginning with East, West, North or South
Arrange under the adjective if it is a part of the official
name, but under the noun if the adjective is merely de-
scriptive. E.g. West Virginia, South Africa (Union), East
St. Louis, North Dakota, class under the adjective; but
Africa, North; Europe, Southern; New York, Western;
United States (East) ; class by the substantive.

> Lippincott's *Gazetteer* will usually decide the question.
> "If the adjective used with the nouns forms a name which is lo-
> cally or administratively a unit, treat as any other distinct place."—
> (Pettee).

316 Suburbs and wards
(a) Description of the suburbs of a large city, including description of the city itself : Class under the city. E.g.
(1) *Rand McNally Chicago guide to the city and environs*
(New York, 1919). (2) *Old roads from the heart of New
York.* By Sarah Comstock (New York, 1917). Class each
under the city.

(b) Description of several suburbs not including the
city : Class under the county or the state in which the region
described is located. E.g. *Rural Pennsylvania in the vicinity
of Philadelphia.* By Samuel Fitch Hotchkin (Philadelphia,
1897).

> The titles of such works should not influence the classifier. E.g.
> one author will describe "Rural Pennsylvania in the vicinity of Phila-
> delphia"; another author may describe the same region as "Mont-
> gomery county."
> L.C. classes *suburbs* as a topic under description of the city. Ex-
> ample cited is classed in suburbs of Philadelphia (F158.68).

(c) History or description of a metropolitan borough of
a city : Class (by subhead) under its own name, if this name
appears in a standard gazetteer.

(d) Works treating of a locality (village, town or
suburb) once independent but now part of a city: Class
(by subhead) usually under the city. E.g. Chelsea, Fulham ;
now parts of London.

Subheads are needed especially in classing the earlier works on the
locality as an independent place.

But if the place has been of local importance or still
maintains a measure of autonomy, class under its own
name. E.g. (1) Brooklyn, now part of New York; (2)
*Hampstead; its historic houses, its literary and artistic
associations.* By Anna Maxwell (London, 1912). Class
under Hampstead, although that is now a part of London.

ANTIQUITIES

317 Archeology vs. History

History, for the classifier, may be taken to comprise primarily literary records (inscribed, written or printed) dealing with past events or conditions of mankind; archeology,
to deal with nonliterary and mostly preliterary relics and
remains of civilized man; prehistoric anthropology, so-
called by some writers, to deal with uncivilized races and
tribes.—(Los Angeles). L.C. classes general archeology in
CC, but antiquities of individual countries are classed in sub-
sections under the history of the country; D.C. classes both
general and local antiquities in 913. L.C. puts prehistoric
archeology (GN) under anthropology; D.C. classes it in
571 under science. E.g. (1) *The lure and lore of archæology.* By Ralph Van Deman Magoffin (Baltimore, 1930).
(2) *The archæology of Cook Inlet, Alaska.* By Frederica
De Laguna (Philadelphia, 1934). (3) *Anthropology and
history.* By William McDougall (London, 1920). (4) *A
handbook of the prehistoric archaeology of Britain.* (Oxford, 1932). (5) *The coming of man, pre-man and prehistoric man.* By George Grant MacCurdy (New York, 1935).

Examples cited are classed: (1) by L.C. in archeology (CC75) ;
so also by D.C. (913). (2) by L.C. in antiquities of Alaska (F906) ;
so also by D.C. (913.798). (3) by L.C. in anthropology (GN27) ; so

also by DC. (572.04). (4) by L.C. in prehistoric remains of Great Britain (GN805); by D.C. in antiquities (913.42). (5) by L.C. in prehistoric archeology (GN738); so also by D.C. (571).

318 Inscriptions

(a) Inscriptions of documentary importance, inscribed on material wrought for the purpose of receiving them: Class by the subject matter of the inscription.—(Los Angeles). E.g. (1) *L'inscription runique du coffret de Mortain.* Par Maurice Cahen . . . (Paris, 1930). (2) *Les inscriptions chinoises de Bodh-Gayâ.* [Par] Édouard Chavannes (Paris, 1896). (3) *Semitic inscriptions.* By Enno Littman (New York, 1904). (4) *Monumental inscriptions in the church and churchyard of St. Mary's, Wimbleton.* [Ed.] by A. W. Hughes Clarke (London, 1934).

Examples cited are classed: (1) by L.C. in runic inscriptions (PD2007.M6); by D.C. in Anglo-Saxon inscriptions (429.17). (2) by L.C. in Buddhism (BL1411.B7); by D.C. in Chinese inscriptions (495.117). (3) by L.C. in Semitic inscriptions (PJ3081). (4) by L.C. in epitaphs (CS436.W595); so also by D.C. (929.5094221), both under genealogy.

(b) Inscriptions engraved on objects that fulfil purposes of their own, or on natural objects not designed to receive them: Class in archeology.—(Los Angeles). E.g. (1) *Seals of ancient Indian style found at Ur.* By C. J. Gadd (London, 1933). (2) *Dighton Rock, a study of written rocks of New England.* By Edmund Burke Delabarre (New York, 1928). (3) *Prehistoric rock pictures in Europe and Africa.* By Leo Frobenius . . . (New York, 1937). (4) *Inscriptions of the Nile monuments.* By G. C. Pier (New York, 1908).

Examples cited are classed: (1) by L.C. in Babylonian iconography (CD5348); by D.C. in seals (736). (2) by L.C. as topic (F74.D45) under history of Massachusetts. (3) by L.C. in *petroglyphs* (GN799.P4) under prehistoric archeology; so also by D.C. (571.73).

(c) Historical inscriptions: Class in history under the country or event commemorated.—(Los Angeles). E.g. (1) *A selection of Greek historical inscriptions to the end of the fifth century B.C.* Ed. by Marcus N. Tod (Oxford, 1933). (2) *The historical inscriptions of southern India.* By Robert Sewell (Madras, 1932). (3) *Prehistoric China.* By James Mellon Menzies (Shanghai, 1917–).

Examples cited are classed: (1) by L.C. in *sources* (DF209.5) under history of Greece; by D.C. in history of Greece (938). (2) by L.C. in history of India (DS441); so also by D.C. (954). (3) by L.C. in antiquities of China (DS715); so also by D.C. (913.31) with alternative in Chinese inscriptions (495.117).

(d) Inscriptions of linguistic or of literary interest: Class in philology, divided by language, e.g. Greek or Latin. E.g. (1) *Through Basque to Minoan, transliterations and translations of the Minoan tablets.* By F. G. Gordon (London, 1931). (2) *Inscriptions de Délos.* Publ. par Félix Durrbach (Paris, 1926-29. 2v.).

Examples cited are classed: (1) by L.C. in Minoan inscriptions (P1035); by D.C. (491.99) under Indo-European languages. (2) by L.C. in *Greek inscriptions* (CN); so also by D.C. (481.7).

Cards for inscriptions, filed in the subject catalog, will bring together material that is scattered by following the above rules. As an inscription is only one form of conveying information or of recording facts, similar to those recorded in books, the matter should take precedence of the form in classification.

"D.C. classes inscriptions according to the special subject illustrated, e.g. philology, history, etc."—(D.C. editors).

319 Historic houses

(a) A work on the history of famous houses or on places associated with famous persons: Class in local history of the place. E.g. *Famous houses and literary shrines of London.* By A. St. John Adcock (London, 1912). Class in history (or antiquities) of London.

L.C. has topic *individual buildings,* in history of the metropolis, e.g. Boston, London, Paris, and classes the original Colonial churches in local history of the American Colonies.

(b) A work on literary shrines, e.g. literary haunts of authors (coffee-houses and inns). See Literary shrines: 314.

(c) A work designed to show the architecture of famous

houses: Class in domestic architecture. E.g. Castles or moated houses of England.
See also Buildings, Individual: 232.

BIOGRAPHY

320 Definition and scope of the class

"There is much divergence in the practice of classing biography. In general there are three methods of dealing with it:

1. To arrange all biography in one straight alphabet arranged by biographee.

2. To arrange in a classed suborder under a general group Biography, as provided for by Dewey.

3. To consider biography, as far as it permits, as subject material, and to class with topic the biography of all individuals whose life work has been a substantial contribution to that topic; to class, for example, the biography of musicians with music, the lives of artists, with art. All classifications do this to some extent. The lives of philosophers invariably are classed with philosophy. The lives and works of the Fathers of the church go with Church Fathers, etc. It is necessary for the classifier to define carefully his own practice in classing biography as subject material. It is not defined by the systems for it is allowable to class biographical material with the history of a topic if no special place is made for it with the topic, e.g. biographies of scientists may be classed in with the history of science.

"Where it is the general practice of the classifiers to distribute biography with topic material, a safe rule to follow is this: If the biographee is identified with any movement or subject important *in itself,* class with that topic, leaving in the general class Biography, only biographies of manysided people who are of no special interest for one subject above another, or biographies whose interest lies only in the appeal of the personal narrative."—(Pettee).

The practice of the Library of Congress in regard to classing biography is as follows: "It is the practice of the Library of Congress to

classify both collected and individual biography with the subject.
. . . The rule is to class the biography of the individual with the
epoch, historical event or locality with which we consider his life
especially identified. . . . Having settled where a man belongs, references are made from other places in the classification where he
might be looked for. . . . A work on some period or event in a man's
career should be classed under the subject."—*Classification*, class
E–F, 2d ed., p.85, note.

321 Biography partially distributed by subject

When biography, whether collected or individual, is partly
kept together and partly distributed through the classification by subject: Class according to the following rules, 322–
351.

The rules to follow, regarding the treatment mostly of individual
biography, will apply to libraries keeping biographies in *one* or in a
few special classes, not distributing them according to the subject,
event or locality with which the life of the biographee is deemed to
have been identified.

322 Artists

Description of the work of an artist in one branch of art,
e.g. sculpture, or book illustration: Class under biography
of the artist, not under the kind of art. E.g. *William Blake's
designs for Gray's poems*. By William Blake (London,
1922). Class with other works on Blake's art.

323 Autobiography

Autobiography, written with the avowed purpose of nar-
rating the history of certain events: Class under those
events; i.e. treat it rather as a personal narrative under the
subject than as a general biography. E.g. *A half century
among the Siamese and the Lao, an autobiography*. By
Daniel McGilvary (New York, 1912). "The story of the
. . . Lao Mission" (preface). Class under missions in
Siam.

Cf. Personal narratives: 345.

324 Bio-bibliography

Class in bibliography; if confined to writers of one nation,
class in national bibliography; if confined to persons of one

class or religious body, class in bibliography of the subject or denomination represented. E.g. Dictionary of English Catholics.

325 Biography vs. Country

(a) Personal narratives covering a single war or other integral group of events: Class under history of the event. E.g. (1) *Drum taps in Dixie; memories of a drummer boy, 1861–1865.* By Delavan S. Miller (Watertown, N.Y., 1905). Class under United States Civil war. (2) *Military reminiscences of the Civil war.* By Jacob Dolson Cox, formerly Major-General (New York, 1900. 2v.).

(b) Narratives covering various events of a long term of years: Class under the biography of the writer. E.g. *Under the old flag; recollections of military operations in the war for the union, the Spanish war, the Boxer rebellion, etc.* By James Harrison Wilson, Brevet Major-General . . . (New York, 1912. 2v.). Class in biography.

Such narratives are written usually by one who is an actor as well as an observer, and hence biography is the main feature.

(c) Relations of a country to an individual foreign ruler, mentioned by name: Class the same as other diplomatic history.

The ruler acts in such matters only as the representative of his country and the personal element is usually quite subordinate.

(d) The times or country during the period of an author, if the biographical element is absent or is introduced merely as a setting for the narrative: Class under the country. E.g. *Horace Walpole's world. A sketch of Whig society under George III.* By Alice Drayton Greenwood (London, 1913). Class under social history of reign of George III.

(e) Description of a country written to illustrate the works of an author: See Literary topography: 279b.

(f) Description of places associated with a certain person or group of persons: Class in biography of the person. E.g. *Homes and haunts of John Ruskin.* By E. T. Cook (London, 1912). Class under Ruskin. Cf. Literary shrines: 314; Historic houses: 319.

326 Biography vs. Event

The share taken by a person in an event or series of events, if the person is sufficiently prominent to be an object of interest in himself, independently of the events in which he took part: Class in biography of the person. E.g. (1) *Le cardinal Louis Aleman, président du concile de Bâle et la fin du grand schisme* . . . [Par Gabriel Pérouse]. (Paris, 1904). While Aleman was identified with the events described, yet the purpose of the book is rather to bring out his action than the events as such. Hence class in biography. (2) *General W. T. Sherman as college president* . . . *early years of Louisiana State University* . . . Ed. by Walter L. Fleming (Cleveland, 1912). While the scope of the book covers only the years of Sherman's life at Louisiana, the main interest of the book will be Sherman. Class in biography.

The line may be somewhat difficult to draw. But to say that all personal narratives should go in biography would remove, e.g., the narratives of service in the United States Civil War from history of that war, and place them under the biography of the unknown private soldiers. On the other hand, to class all biographical material—short of complete lives—by the subject, will remove from biography many works of as much, if not more, personal than topical interest and value. Speaking generally, the narratives of part taken by *leaders* in events will ordinarily go in biography, the narratives of *observers*, taking a subordinate share of action, will go under the topic.

The University of California classes all such works in biography. The practice of the Library of Congress is stated in section 320.

327 Biography vs. Subject

(a) In case of doubt between personal biography and author's avowed intent to illustrate a subject, follow the latter in classing the work. E.g. *The birth of the English Church; Saint Augustine of Canterbury.* By Sir Henry H. Howorth (London, 1913). "The story of the Pope's English mission" (preface). Class under English Church in preference to biography of Saint Augustine, who is but the central figure, not the subject.

(b) Personal recollections of two or more places: Class

under the biography of the writer. E.g. *Other days. Recollections of rural England and old Virginia, 1860-1880.* By A. G. Bradley (London, 1913). Class under biography of the author.

The only alternative is to select one place and neglect the other. By putting the book in biography, we conserve all the subject-matter under a heading where it is not out of place in any case.

(c) When a work includes both life and works of an author: Class with works, when the life occupies a subordinate place, e.g. one volume in a set of several volumes. Class in biography, when the life is interwoven with the works or when the works are included not in their entirety but in sections.

(d) Biography of a writer accompanied by selections from his writings: Class by the predominant feature.— (New York State Library). E.g. *Chamisso, a sketch of his life and work; with specimens of his poetry and . . . text of "Salas y Gomez."* By Karl Lentzner (London, 1893). Class under German literature.

328 Collective biography

(a) A collection of biographies: Class by the intent of the author; in other words, if the author has selected certain persons as typifying or illustrating a subject, treat the work as dealing with that subject no matter who the individuals may be. E.g. *Pioneer humanists.* By John M. Robertson (London, 1907). Class under biography of humanists, although Bacon, Hobbes, Spinoza (philosophers) are included.

(b) Collective biography, if scattered by system under history of countries and under subjects: Class strictly by period or topic. E.g. (1) Lives of the Westminster divines. Class with Westminster assembly. (2) Collective biography of parliamentarians. Class with history of Parliament, not mixed with other more general political biography.

Biographies contained in so-called *legislative* handbooks often cover administrative and judicial, as well as legislative, departments of the state.

(c) Groups like "Lincoln and his friends," "George II and his ministers": Class as individual biography—Lincoln or George II—or as collective, according as the book is intended to illustrate one man or many men; i.e. whether the other men are introduced to exhibit the character of the central figure, or the individuals of the group are described separately but less fully than the central figure.

329 Correspondence

(a) Correspondence between two persons: Class under the first named on the title-page unless the second correspondent is of unquestionably more importance. E.g. *The correspondence of Thomas Carlyle and Ralph Waldo Emerson, 1834–1872.* Ed. by C. E. Norton (Boston, 1899. 2v.). Class under Carlyle.

Yet there are cases where the position of the names has been determined for reasons of social or intellectual preeminence and not because the book contains as much if not more about the first named author. The connection of the editor with the book may indicate the real intent of the book. E.g. Correspondence of Lord Coleridge and Ellis Yarnall is edited by Yarnall's son, and is a contribution primarily to his father's life.

(b) Correspondence between two persons regarding one of them principally: Class under the one who is the subject of the correspondence.

(c) Personal letters: Class in biography.

(d) Personal letters that treat of one topic: Class by that topic. E.g. *Letters from high latitudes.* By Lord Dufferin (London, 1857). Class in travel in Scandinavia.

(e) Letters of kings and other hereditary rulers: Class in biography, unless biography of rulers is a subdivision of the history of a country.

(f) Letters of literary men and women: Class in literary biography.

The alternative would be to class with the works of writers.

330 Diaries and journals

(a) A journal kept by an individual during a war or period of history or illustrating the progress of events in a place: Class under the history of the war or locality. E.g. *Diary of the besieged resident in Paris.* By Henry Labouchere (London, 1872). Class under Siege of Paris.

The author catalog will sufficiently bring out the writer's connection with the journal.

Cf. Autobiography: 323.

(b) Journals of literary men and women: Class with their biography.

The alternative would be to class with their works, which some classifiers may prefer to do.

(c) A diary covering the period of a lifetime or not confined to one group of events: Class under biography of the writer.

(d) A diary covering a single war, a political movement, a literary coterie, or the like: Class under the subject, unless the writer of the diary or journal is an actor of prominence in the events. E.g. *The journal of John Stevens, containing a brief account of the war in Ireland, 1689–1691.* Ed. by the Rev. Robert H. Murray (Oxford, 1912). Class under Irish history because the author was not a prominent participant.

In the latter case systems may provide for such biographies by a subdivision under the subject, e.g. personal narratives of the Civil War. If not, class in biography.

(e) A diary or journal illustrating the history or manners and customs of a period: Class under the period or the topic unless the writer is an *actor* of prominence in the time; if so, class under biography. E.g. *Journal of the plague year.* By Daniel Defoe. Class in history of the plague in London. But *Diary of George Washington,* class in biography.

The reason for this ruling is that many autobiographical narratives undoubtedly illustrate certain periods of human history, but to class them there would vacate the biography of certain individuals.

(f) Official diaries: Class by the subject, not in biography of the individual author. E.g. *The official diary of Lieutenant-general Adam Williamson, deputy-lieutenant of the Tower of London, 1722–1747.* Ed. by John Charles Fox (London, 1912). Class under Tower of London.

(g) Diaries of miscellaneous content and those covering much or all of the writer's lifetime: Class in biography.

(h) Diaries of obscure persons: Class by topic, especially if printed as illustrative of the topic or time. E.g. *Diary of Anna Green Winslow, a Boston school girl of 1771* (Boston, 1894). Class in history of Boston.

331 Individual biography

(a) Class individual biography together in one alphabet or scatter by the subject, according as the system provides partially or wholly. Cf. sections 320-321.

There is far more reason for grouping lives of individual artists, musicians and printers with art, music and printing than for attempting to classify every biography by the appropriate field of the subject's career.

The question of whether to break up individual biography by subject—either partially or completely—depends very much upon the use to which biography is put in a library. If it is used for reference purposes, there is much more reason for bringing lives of certain persons close to the subjects associated with them, than if the section of biography is used for general reading in the same way as fiction or travel.

(b) Biography of a person considered under one phase of his character or work: Class under biography, not under the topic concerned. E.g. *Thomas Jefferson as an architect and a designer of landscapes.* By William Alexander Lambeth and Warren H. Manning (Boston and New York, 1913). Class under Jefferson.

A man's character is indivisible and special features should not be treated in classification abstractly. As usual, the special library will treat this, as well as general biographies of the person, according to the needs of the library.

332 Individual biography of actors

Biography, memoirs, recollections and similar works about individual actors and actresses: Class under their biography, wherever it may be placed in the system, not under the history of the theaters with which they have been connected. E.g. *Stage confidences; talks about players and play acting.* By Clara Morris (Boston, 1902). Class under Clara Morris.

Personality in the case of persons of this class is always pronounced and is more the center of interest than the scenes of their careers, e.g. Henry Irving, Edmund Kean.

333 Individual biography of founders of religions

Individual biography of founders of religions: Class under the religion.—(Los Angeles). E.g. (1) *Mohammed, the man and his faith.* By Tor Andræ; tr. by Theophil Menzel (New York, 1936). (2) *The life of Mahomet.* By Émile Dermenghem (London, 1930). (3) *Jesus, a new biography.* By Shirley Jackson Case (Chicago, 1927). (4) *Christ of the countryside.* By Malcolm Dana (Nashville, 1937).

D.C. provides for classification of founders of religion under either biography (922) or religion (200).

The reason for this rule, which may be followed even by libraries that do not ordinarily scatter biography by subject, is stated by Los Angeles thus: "It is frequently impossible to distinguish between the biography of the founders of the religions and the early history."

Cf. Definition and scope of biography: 320.

334 Individual biography of missionaries

If individual lives are classed by subject: "Class with the missionary field with which the missionary is identified."— (Pettee).

335 Individual biography of musicians

(a) Biography of musicians (composers, performers) and criticism of their works collectively: Class as biography.

(b) Criticism of the compositions of a single composer when limited to a single type of composition. See Musical criticism: 242b.

336 Individual biography of rulers

(a) Biography of kings and other hereditary rulers: Class under the history of their reigns.

Detailed classifications will have, under the reign or period of prominent rulers, a subdivision for biographies, e.g. Napoleon I.

(b) Biography of elective rulers: Class in biography.

Emperors of the Holy Roman Empire, although elective to some extent, should be treated like hereditary rulers.

337 Individual biography of slaves

(a) Biography of slaves who, after emancipation, have distinguished themselves: Class in biography. E.g. (1) *Toussaint-L'Ouverture.* Par Michel Vaucaire (Paris, 1930). (2) *A brief biography of Booker Washington.* By Anson Phelps Stokes [Hampton, Va., 1936].

Examples cited are classed: (1) by L.C. in *biography of Toussaint-L'Ouverture* (F1923.T96) under history of Haiti; by D.C. in biography of Haitian rulers (923.27294). (2) by L.C. in *biography of American negroes* (E185.97.W273) under U.S. history; by D.C. in biography of American educators (923.773).

(b) Biography of slaves whose life in slavery simply illustrates the conditions under slavery: Class in slavery. E.g. *Thirty years a slave, autobiography of Louis Hughes.* (Milwaukee, 1897).

338 Individual biography of two persons

Class under the first named unless the second is unquestionably a person of greater importance. E.g. *Coleridge and Wordsworth in the west country.* By Professor Knight (London, 1913). Class under Coleridge.

339 Individual biography of wives of famous men

Class (or alphabet) the life of a woman under her own name, even though she be associated in life with some king or other prominent person. E.g. *The wife of General Bonaparte.* By Joseph Turquam; tr. . . . by Violette Montagu (London, 1912). Class under Josephine, empress of the French.

The subject catalog will bring out the associations of her life. By treating the subject of the biography independently, books about her are disengaged from others treating of kings and other persons from a different point of view. Another reason for classing a woman under her own name is the impossibility of making a clear and consistent distinction between biographies "more useful" under the lady and those "more useful" under her husband, son or other relative's name. L.C. classes the Bonaparte family (DC216) under history of France.

340 Influence of a person on events or institutions

Class under the person in biography unless the factor influenced is definite and specific. E.g. *Thomas Jefferson; his permanent influence on American institutions.* By John Sharp Williams (New York, 1913). Class under biography of Jefferson. But class *Influence of George III on the development of the* [British] *constitution,* by A. Mervyn Davies (London, 1921) under British constitutional history.

The personal element will usually be prominent and pervasive in any treatment of a person's relation to a given thing. In a system that distributes individual biography through the classification, as the Library of Congress largely does, the rule will in some cases coalesce with the exception.

341 Influence of one person upon another

(a) Class under the biography of the person affected. E.g. *The influence of Grenville on Pitt's foreign policy, 1787–1798.* By Ephraim Douglass Adams (Washington, 1904). Class under Pitt. See also Influence of one writer upon another: 292b.

(b) Class under the topic if limited and definite in scope. E.g. *The influence of Cicero upon Augustine in the development of his oratorical theory for the training of the ecclesiastical orator.* By James Burnette Eskridge (Menasha, Wis., 1912). Class under preaching.

342 Interviews, Conversations

(a) Interviews or conversations of famous or prominent persons: Class under the subject unless the import of the interview is so personal that the speaker is really the subject. E.g. *Conversation of James Northcote, R. A., with James Ward on art and artists.* Ed. by Ernest Fletcher (London, 1901). Class under art.

(b) Interviews in which the personality and work of the person interviewed form the subject of conversation: Class in biography. E.g. *Art.* By Auguste Rodin. From the French of Paul Gsell, by Mrs. Romilly Fedden (London, 1912). Largely Rodin's art and illustrated by his own work. Class in art biography.

343 Literary biography

> If individual literary biography is classed by subject, the acts of the man and the events with which he was connected are to be considered more than the topics upon which he wrote. E.g. *Life and letters of Ernst Curtius* has much of interest upon the period in which Curtius lived, but little on the history of Greece, upon which he wrote.

344 Memoirs

(a) Autobiographical memoirs: Class in biography unless the historical aspect decidedly predominates.

(b) Memoirs of prominent men and women: Class in biography, unless they are explicitly stated to be memoirs of historical events, reigns, "mémoires pour servir," etc. E.g. Life of Napoleon. But *Mémoires du duc de Luynes sur la cour de Louis XV* (Paris, 1860–65. 17v.). Class in French history.

> Unless all individual biography is classed by the system under the subject illustrated, memoirs should not be excluded from the class of biography as they are often the best or the only first-hand materials for the life of the person.

345 Personal narratives

(a) Class in biography if the writers are prominent enough to render the personal element in the book foremost; otherwise their narratives are of value only for the subject.

> Examples are the usual "personal narratives" of soldiers in war, reminiscences of pioneer life, travel in foreign countries, and the like. In case of doubt, biography should be chosen for a narrative covering the whole life of the narrator; otherwise the subject determines the class.
>
> Diaries and letters are usually classed in biography; but the diary of a soldier in the Civil war has more significance for history than for biography, the reason being that the author is (usually) unknown to fame. On the other hand, the diary left by a general might go in biography on account of the prominence of the author. Travels are personal events for the authors of them; but the personal data given are usually of less importance than the description of scenes visited.

Cf. Autobiography: 323.

(b) Personal narratives of travel or history: Class under the country or place, not in biography. E.g. *Impressions of*

America and the American churches, from journal of the Rev. G. Lewis (Edinburgh, 1845). Class in travel.

The intent of the author is usually to furnish information about the place, and the interest for the reader will not be in the narrator save in the case of singularly prominent persons.

(c) A personal narrative of service during a war in *one* regiment: Class under personal narratives of that war in preference to the section of regimental histories. E.g. *A narrative of service with the Third Wisconsin Infantry.* By Julian Wisner Hinkley (Madison, 1912).

The reasons are: (1) Every narrator serves in some regiment and most of them in only one during a war; (2) the narrative being personal, naturally gravitates to other similar narratives in which the name of the regiment is not mentioned and hence is usually unknown. But if the work is expressly stated to be a history of the regiment, follow the intent of the author.

(d) Naval service in a war: Class in naval history of the war.

(e) European war (1914–18): Class with the army, country, branch of the service, or campaign with which the writer was connected.

346 Personal opinions

(a) A work giving the personal impressions and opinions of some public character: Class under his biography. E.g. *Opinions of Anatole France,* recorded by Paul Gsell (New York, 1922).

(b) Views of a given writer on a certain topic: Class under the topic. E.g. *Bayle et la tolérance.* Par Lucien Dubois (Paris, 1902).

This case differs from that cited in section 340 in which a person's actions or influence upon events is concerned.

Cf. also Author's opinions as subjects in literature: 267.

(c) History of a person's opinions: Class in biography of the person concerned, especially when some biographical matter enters in, except when dealing with a special subject. E.g. Newman's *Apologia pro vita sua* . . . with introduction, by Wilfrid Ward. (Oxford ed.; London, 1913).

A prominent name placed in a title to attract attention and promote sale of a book must not be mistaken for the subject of the book. E.g. *The sisters of Lady Jane Grey* has nothing to do with that well-known character; nor does *Bismarck's pen* deal primarily with Bismarck but with Heinrich Abeken, whose life was by no means *only* the "pen." Personality, if prominent enough to write about at all, has usually an interest of its own which justifies classification under it.

347 Personal relations

(a) The relations of two persons or groups of persons to each other: Class according to the personal importance of the parties concerned, if no other canon of classification applies, the intent of the author being usually to contribute something to the history of the more important party. E.g. (1) *A Royalist family, Irish and French (1689–1789) and Prince Charles Edward* [By Louis La Trémoille] ; tr. by A. G. Murray Macgregor (Edinburgh, 1904). Class under Charles Edward Stuart, the Young Pretender. (2) *Dr. Johnson and Fanny Burney, being the Johnsonian passages from the works of Mme. D'Arblay.* Ed. by C. B. Tinker (London, 1912). Class under biography of Johnson, not of Mme. D'Arblay, because the intent of the editor is to select only passages relating to Johnson.

(b) A controversy or quarrel of two persons over some common cause: Class under the subject concerned. E.g. The controversy between Bossuet and Fénélon regarding Quietism. Class under Quietism.

(c) Narratives of duels. See Duels: 169.

348 Polemical biography

Polemical biography is biography of persons selected as examples of religious faith, political opinion, literary school, and the like, written usually by either an adherent or an opponent of the group exemplified.

Collective polemical biography: Class under the faith, party or school represented.

The intent of the author in such cases is to illustrate the character and attainments of adherents of that church or party. In case of conflict between religious and scientific biography, choose religious if the work in hand is polemical.

349 Race biography

Collective biography of men of one race: Class rather by the country in which they lived than by the country of their origin, e.g. biography of Scotsmen in Canada, class under Canadian, not Scottish biography.

The reasons are: (1) that their lives are naturally more identified with events in their adopted country than with their native land; and (2) classification according to racial affinities should be used only for family history and for ethnology.

350 Race history, local

History of men of one race in a locality: Class in local history, not with history of the race in a country. E.g. *Chronicles of the Scotch-Irish settlement in Virginia* (Rosslyn, Va., 1912–13. 3v.). Class under Virginia, not under the Scotch-Irish in the United States.

The local genealogical elements in such works, and the intimate relation to the history of the locality, are too strong to be neglected for the sake of the racial affinities.

351 Women

(a) Biographies of women eminent in special fields: Class under the subject, not in general biography.—(John Crerar Library).

(b) Fields and aspects of women's activities: Class under subject, not under woman.

The John Crerar Library rule is: "Class biographies of women under the special field in which they are known, not under subject Women. Class books about women, as, labor of women, education of women, under the primary subject of the book, not under Women."

GENEALOGY

The term genealogy covers family histories, registers of births, marriages and deaths, and vital records. If careful separation between family histories, town records, and the local history of landed property be deemed unnecessary, most works that largely bring in families by name will be classed in genealogy, the general and frequent introduction of names of settlers into the book drawing it to genealogy more than to local history proper or to land (under economics).

352 Church records

Registers of births, marriages and deaths kept by churches, or records largely made up of such items: Class in genealogy or local history, not in local *church* history. E.g. *Records of the First Church in Beverly, Massachusetts, 1667–1772.* Copied by William P. Upham . . . (Salem, 1905). Class in genealogy of Beverly.

The University of California classes church registers in local secular history; so also does L.C.

353 Family history

(a) Several generations, including an account of some especially prominent member of it: Class under family history. E.g. *The ancestry of Abraham Lincoln.* By J. Henry Lea and J. R. Hutchinson (Boston, 1909). Class as Lincoln genealogy.

(b) Biography of a prominent or public character, including notices of his family: Class under biography of the character. E.g. (1) *The Brontës; life and letters.* By Clement Shorter (London, 1908–09. 2v.). Class under Charlotte Brontë. (2) *Ellen Terry and her sisters.* By T. Edgar Pemberton (London, 1902). Class under Ellen Terry.

Examples cited are classed (1) by L.C. in individual writers—Brontës (PR4168) under English literature. (2) in biography of actresses (PN2287) under drama.

(c) In cases of doubt: Class in family history only when three or more generations are mentioned and at some length in each case.

(d) Art or literary work of members of a single family: Class as collective art or literary biography. E.g. *The Wood family of Burslem, a brief biography of those of its members who were sculptors, modellers and potters.* By Frank Falkner (London, 1912). Class under potters, or Burslem pottery.

354 Family history vs. Town history

(a) A book treating both town history and genealogy of settlers in the town: Class in local history as the more inclusive of the two topics.

(b) Town histories composed mostly of family records: Class in genealogy. E.g. *History of Montville, Conn.* By Henry A. Baker (Hartford, 1896). Only twelve per cent history; class in genealogy of Montville.

The New York State Library classes all town histories in local history, irrespective of genealogical content. L.C. classes local genealogy with local history.

355 Family history vs. Peerage

Genealogy of a noble or titled family: Class under the family name, not under the title or under the domain. E.g. *The rulers of Strathspey; a history of the lairds of Grant and earls of Seafield.* By the earl of Cassillis (Inverness, 1911). Class under Ogilvie-Grant family.

Example cited is classed by L.C. in *family history* (CS479.O5) under genealogy of Scotland.

356 Family history vs. Religious bodies

(a) Collective genealogy of members of the same religious body, e.g. Huguenots: Class in genealogy. E.g. *Publications* of the Huguenot Society of London. Consist mostly of registers of parishes in Great Britain showing Huguenot families.

A difficult case to treat otherwise than illogically. Genealogy belongs near biography. But if the biography, at least the collective biography, is classed with the subject illustrated—as is done in some classifications—then the genealogy should go there too, for it is the biography of families. But the subject matter of genealogy is so far removed from the subject supposed to be illustrated that all genealogy is better kept together. The history of the family of an individual Huguenot is of less importance to the historian than to the genealogist. Hence family history is to be preferred to religious history.

(b) Collective genealogy of a town or locality settled largely by persons of the same religious faith: Class under local genealogy.

New York State Library classes in local history; so does L.C.

357 Literary families

The history of several members of a literary family: Class in literary biography, not in genealogy, especially if the intent of the author is literary. E.g. (1) *The three Brontës*. By May Sinclair (London, 1912). Best placed with biographies of Charlotte Brontë.

358 Genealogy vs. Political history

The history of a family concerned in public affairs: Class in genealogy, even if the part taken by the family is prominent in history. But distinguish such works from histories of dynasties. E.g. Stuarts; Bonapartes.

This rule is analogous to the section relating to Biography vs. Event: 326.

359 Local landholders

Lists of local landholders and householders: Class in local history, not in landed property (economics). E.g. *The home lots of the early settlers of the Providence plantations*. By Charles Wyman Hopkins (Providence, 1886). Class in history of Providence, R. I.

This type is mostly material of historical interest, and does not, of course, include directories of cities.

360 Names

(a) Dictionaries and gazetteers of names, general in scope: Class with other dictionaries or gazetteers of general information.—(Los Angeles). E.g. Lippincott's *Gazetteer*.

(b) Works on place names and family names of a special locality: Class in local genealogy or local history. E.g. *Yorkshire place names as recorded in the Yorkshire Domesday book, 1086*. By J. Horsfall Turner (Bingley, n.d.). Class in Yorkshire names, not with the Domesday book, the source.

L.C. classes personal and family names in genealogy (CS2300–) and place names in history (D,E,F) by locality; D.C. classes names of persons and places in genealogy (929.4).

Example cited is classed by L.C. in history of Yorkshire (DA670.Y6).

HISTORICAL PERIODS AND TOPICS

361 Crusades

Histories of principalities and kingdoms founded during the crusades: Class in history of the locality, under the crusades. E.g. The Latin Kingdom of Jerusalem.

In most systems, crusades are grouped under universal history. Local works should not be mixed with the general histories. Accounts of sieges may be treated by the usual rule of grouping under wars and be classed under the history of the crusade in which they occurred. E.g. Siege of Acre.

362 Indians of America

Indians of America as a class include all aborigines of the two Americas, comprising the tribes of primitive culture and the semi-civilized peoples of Mexico and South America. The Mound Builders and the Eskimo are included.

(a) Works dealing in a general way with the Indians of North America since the discovery by Columbus: Class under history of America. E.g. (1) *The North American Indians.* By Rose A. Palmer [New York, 1934]. (2) *American Indians, first families of the Southwest.* By J. F. Huckel (5th ed.; Albuquerque, 1934). (3) *The Indians of to-day.* By G. B. Grinnell (New York, 1900).

(b) Works on the aboriginal languages of America: Class in language. E.g. (1) *The native languages of California.* By Roland B. Dixon . . . (n.p., 1903?). (2) *Cuadro descriptivo y comparativo de las lenguas indígenas de México.* Por Francisco Pimentel (2. ed.; México, 1874–75. 3v.).

(c) Works on pre-Columbian antiquities: Class in aboriginal antiquities of America.—(Los Angeles). E.g. (1)*History of America before Columbus.* By P. de Roo (Philadelphia, 1900. 2v.). (2) *L'Amérique précolombienne, essai sur l'origine de sa civilisation.* Par Charles A. N. Gagnon (Quebec, 1908). (3) *Ancient Americans.* By E. C. Davis (New York, 1931).

Examples cited are classed by L.C. in *archeology* of the American Indians (E61) under history of America.

(d) Works on the antiquities, history, ethnology, customs, and religion of the aborigines of Mexico, Central America and the separate countries of South America: Class under country in history or by subject, according to system. E.g. (1) *Ancient life in Mexico and Central America.* By Edgar J. Hewett (Indianapolis, 1936). (2) *Mexico before Cortez, an account of the daily life, religion and ritual of the Aztecs and kindred peoples.* By J. Eric Thompson (New York, 1933). (3) *Estaban a punto de extinguirse los pueblos de Anáhuac a la llegada de los Españoles?* [Por] Raquel García Méndez y Desgardin (México, 1935). (4) *Indians of southern Mexico, an ethnographic album.* By Frederick Starr (Chicago, 1899). (5) *A history of American anthropology.* [By] Panchanan Mitra (Calcutta, 1933).

L.C. classes all material on the American Indians (E51–) under history of America, except languages (PM); "D.C. provides for bringing together all works on Indians of America under 970.1–.6 for Indians in general and North American, and similarly under 980.1–.6 for South American."—(D.C. editors). Queens Borough classes the arts of the American Indians with the specific art, and Indian costumes in costume.

363 Fourth of July orations

(a) Fourth of July orations containing local history: Class under the history of the town.

(b) Fourth of July orations dealing with the general significance of the day: Class under United States history. Cf. Festival and holiday addresses: 21.

The New York State Library classes these under United States history. Queens Borough "classes Fourth of July orations dealing with the general significance of the day in 394 [customs], the history value is so likely to be slight."

364 Localities settled by one sect

Secular history of localities settled or now occupied by members of one church or religious sect: Class in local history. E.g. (1) *The Belgians (Walloons) first settlers in New York and in the middle states* (New York, 1925). Class in

Walloons under history of New York State. (2) The Pilgrim Fathers; Puritans in Massachusetts; Huguenots in South Carolina, are other examples.

365 State and county together

The history of a state of the Union, county or city of a state, accompanied by a sketch of the larger political division in which it is located (United States or state) : Class under the smaller division. E.g. *Historical encyclopedia of Illinois . . . and history of Evanston* (Chicago, 1906. 2v.). The history of Illinois is duplicated with each city and county in this enclycopedia of the state. Class under Evanston.

This rule will not apply, however, to school books "especially adapted" to a certain state, in which the matter of the book is primarily general, as in a general geography.

Index

Medical bacteriology, 198b
Medicine, sport, 199
Medieval church history, 85–86
Medieval romances, 171
Memoirs, 344
  of diplomats, 110
Metals, 224
Method vs. Subject-matter, 14
Metrical translations, 272
Mexican antiquities, aboriginal,
  362d
Military aeronautics, 213
Military biography, local, 153
Military engineering, 211–213
Military map-reading, 212
Military science, 145–155
Militia regiments, 147b
Mining engineering, 210
Miscellany in periodical form, 263
Missionaries, individual biography,
  334
Modeling (display of garments),
  121
Modification of rules for special
  needs, 6
Monastic chronicles, 88
Monographs issued by periodicals,
  33d
  issued serially, 27d-27e
Monuments, battlefield, 150
Mountain fauna, 194e
Moving pictures, 252
Municipal documents, 141
Municipal ownership, 137a
Municipalities, Roman, 142
Muscular exercise, physiology and
  psychology of, 120
Music, 239–250
  arrangements, 250
  definition and scope, 239
  dramatic, 243
  incidental, 241
  vs. Drama, 241
  vs. Poetry, 240
Musical criticism, 242
Musicians, individual biography,
  335
  criticism of their compositions,
  335b
Mythological characters in literature, 268b

Names, 360
  in statistical reports, 97b
Narratives, personal, 345
National bibliography vs. National
  printing, 51b
  vs. Subject bibliography, 50
National constitutions, 134
National economic emergency meas-
  ures, 143
National planning, 118a
National political ideals, 102
Nationality of authors, 285
Natural history, 189
  expeditions, 176
Natural resources, conservation,
  118b
Naval history, 156
Naval science, 156–157
Navy, 156
Nazi régime, 100
Negro authors, 282
Newspapers, 23
Normal colleges, 164

Opera, 243
  librettos, 244
Opinions, personal, 346
Origin of political institutions, 114
Original manuscripts, 58
Outbuildings for animals, 226
Overtures, operas, 243b
  orchestral music, 243e
Ownership, public, 137

Pageants, 170, 241e
Painting, 236
Paintings, portrait, 238c
Pamphlets, 24
Papal letters or documents, 90b
Papal relations with countries, 90
Parishes, 83
Parties, political, 116–117
Patois, specimens 256e,
Patriotic society publications, 301
Peerage vs. Family history, 355
Periodical miscellany, 263
Periodicals, 33
  denominational, 89
  weekly, issued by newspapers,
  23a–23c
Periods of time, 39–40

Personal accounts of travel, 310a
Personal letters, 329
Personal narratives of a war, 325a
Personal opinions, 346
Personal recollections, 327b
Personal relations, 347
Persons as subjects in literature, 268
  poems on, 274
Philology, 255–259
  definition and scope, 255
Philosophers, works of, 67
Philosophic ideas in literature, 68
Philosophy, 66–69
  definition and scope, 66
  in literature, 269
  in poetry, 273
  of individual writers, 294
Photoelectric cells, 185
Photography, 187
Photoplays, 252c
Physical methods in biological study, 14b
Physical theories, applications of, 197
Physics, 181
  atomic, 182
  mathematical, 181b
Physiological psychology, 72
Physiology of labor and muscular exercise, 120
Pianoforte music, 247
Place names, 360b
  arrangement of, 315
Places, bibliography, 49
  literary history of, 279
Planning, city, 139
  economic, 118
Plants, edible and nonedible, 220
  evolution of, 192b
  geographical distribution, 193a
  single species, 193b
Plays, arranged for acting, 276c
  for moving pictures, 252c
  for radio broadcasting, 215d
  incidental music for, 241
  prose renderings, 276d
  used for librettos, 244c
Plots, 296
Poems on persons, 274
Poems, prose renderings of, 276d
  set to music, 241c

Poetry, 271–275
  for public readings, 264
  philosophy in, 273
  vs. Music, 240
Polemical biography, 348
Political communism, 123b
Political documents, 96
Political history, 302
  vs. Genealogy, 358
Political ideals, national, 102
Political ideas in history, 300
Political institutions, origin of, 114
Political opinions of theologians, 81
Political parties, 116–117
Political policy, 104
Political science, 98–106
Political theory, of a special country or school, history of, 101
Political unions, 108
Politics, 303
Population, statistics, 97a
Portraits, 238
Precious stones, 234
Princeps editions of ancient manuscripts, 59g
Principalities founded during the crusades, 361
Printing presses, early, publications of, 62d
Printing vs. Bibliography, 51
Private libraries, 57
Professional ethics, 78
Prohibited books, 64
Prose for public readings, 264
Prospecting, geophysical, 210
Psychology, 70–77
  definition and scope, 70
  of animals, 195
  of events or of phenomena, 75
  of industry, 77
  of labor and muscular exercise, 120
  of politics and history, 76
Public finance, 124a
Public libraries, 56
Public ownership, 137
Public works, 138

Quantum mechanics of chemical reactions, 184

Subject bibliography, 52
vs. National bibliography, 50
Subject vs. Biography, 327
vs. Method, 14
Subjects, coordinated, 15d
history of, 12
in relation, 15
limited by country, 42
limited by time, 39
literary history of, 47
treated genetically (i.e. as to origin), 11
treated in literature, 270
treated in poetry, 275
Suburbs, 316
Suffrage, 105
Surgery, 201
Surgical treatment of injuries, 199b

Tactics, 154
Taxation, local, 124b–124c
Teaching of individual subjects, 163
Technicians, books for, 38
mathematics for, 177d
Technology, 196–226
Tempering of metals, 224b
Thanksgiving Day addresses, 21, 29
Theater, 251–253
vs. Drama, 251
Theatrical travel, 253
Theologians, political opinions of, 81
Theological point of view, 80
Theoretical-applied science, 197
Theory of a subject treated locally, 43
Things as subjects in literature, 270
Time divisions, 39–41
in history, 309
vs. Local divisions, 309
Time-measuring instruments, 180
Tools, 207–209
Topics. See Subjects
Topography, literary, 279
Tours, 254

Town history vs. Family history, 354
Traditions in literature, 299
Trailers for automobiles, 214
Translations, 30, 259
metrical, 272
Travel, 310–316
theatrical, 253
vs. Ethnology, 191b
Travels for research, 310c
Travels of distinguished personages, 310b
Treaties, 129
Treaty outcomes, 130
Tribes, 191
Types of literary material, special, 17–30
Typical examples (science), 190

Unemployment insurance, 160c
Unions, political, 108
Useful arts, 196–226

Vacuum tubes, 186b
Ventilation of buildings, 216a
Veterinarians, anatomy for, 202
Vocal scores, 250
Vocational guidance, 162
Vocations for women, 162c

Wards, 316
Wars, 148
diplomatic history of, 111
Welding, 206
Welfare, 158–160
Wildlife, conservation of, 118b
Wives of famous men, individual biography, 339
Women, activities, 351b
biography, 351a
vocations, 162c
Women's colleges, 165
Woven fabrics, 235
Writer, intent of, 4

Zoology, 194